THE
BRITISH
MUSEUM
PUZZLE
BOOK

THE
BRITISH
MUSEUM
PUZZLE
BOOK

DR GARETH MOORE

With over 250 illustrations

Thames &Hudson

The British Museum

First published in the United Kingdom in 2023 by
Thames & Hudson Ltd, 181A High Holborn, London WC1V 7QX,
in collaboration with the British Museum

The British Museum Puzzle Book © 2023 The Trustees
of the British Museum/Thames & Hudson Ltd, London

Puzzle text and graphics by Dr Gareth Moore and Laura Jayne Ayres
All other text © 2023 The Trustees of the British Museum

Images © 2023 The Trustees of the British Museum,
unless otherwise stated on pages 247–255

Designed by Dan Prescott

British Library Cataloguing-in-Publication Data
A catalogue record for this book is available from
the British Library

ISBN 978-0-500-48091-5

Printed in Slovenia by GPS Group

MIX
Paper | Supporting
responsible forestry
FSC www.fsc.org **FSC® C118234**

For more information about the Museum and its collection,
please visit **britishmuseum.org**.

Be the first to know about our new releases,
exclusive content and author events by visiting
thamesandhudson.com
thamesandhudsonusa.com
thamesandhudson.com.au

Contents

Introduction

The British Museum is one of the world's best-known and most-visited museums, with a collection of more than 8 million objects from across the globe. Founded in 1753, it is the world's oldest national public museum and, since opening its doors in 1759, has welcomed 'all studious and curious persons' to explore the history of the world through its collection.

The Museum is an enormous place, with more than seventy galleries that explore the extraordinary diversity of human cultures, from small communities to vast empires. The many forms of expression human beings have given to every aspect of life are explored in the Museum's galleries, revealing how closely we are all interconnected.

The artefacts housed by the Museum span 2 million years of human history. Many were taken from or purchased in regions previously under British colonial rule and then sold, donated or bequeathed to the Museum. Others were acquired through excavations, sales and bequests by collectors. Curators continue to acquire objects and are engaged in active research into the collection, including how the objects were originally obtained. Researchers collaborate with the Museum's scientists and academic and community partners internationally. These collection stories are shared with the world through gallery displays, temporary exhibitions, publications, public programming, the Museum's website and social media. They can also be explored by searching the Collection online database.

Although they can only scratch the surface of the Museum's extensive collection, each of the puzzles in this book is based around one or more of the Museum's many artefacts – or, in the case of the first chapter, around the history of the Museum itself. Subsequent chapters focus on items associated with everyday living, before moving on to those that evoke the animal kingdom, or relate to the myths and magical beliefs of different cultures. The penultimate chapter looks at how the Museum's artefacts track the development of the written word, while the book concludes by considering the many magnificent historical treasures that are on display for the benefit of all.

The puzzles are hugely varied, but none require you to be a historian. Often they include a series of logic- or word-based deductions that, once made, will reveal a fact about an object. In general, therefore, you won't require any specialist knowledge to solve them. Occasionally, however, and usually only after completing the main part of a puzzle, you are asked to match artefacts to words or descriptions, and in these cases the intent is simply that you have a go: you are of course not expected to be an expert in all the many areas covered by this book. Full answers are provided at the back, along with full picture captions containing information that wouldn't fit – or would give away the answer – if placed directly alongside the images that accompany the questions.

Enjoy the puzzles, and good luck!

1

The British Museum

The British Museum brings together the whole of human history under one roof. Founded during the Enlightenment, the Museum was the first of its kind – open to everyone to engage with a unique collection of objects. Originally, visits were by appointment only and during limited visiting hours; from the 1830s onwards, however, regulations were changed and the Museum became truly open and freely accessible to all. Today, more than 6 million local and international visitors are welcomed at the Museum every year, while extensive touring exhibitions and a loans programme ensure that millions more are able to see objects from the collection at venues across the UK and worldwide.

1. Who's Who?

The entrance to the British Museum is crowned with a remarkable pediment, designed by Sir Richard Westmacott and unveiled in 1852. Several human and animal figures are shown, representing – from left to right as you view the sculptures – the different stages on humanity's journey from a primitive existence to civilization.

Use the clues on page 10 to determine the correct order of the figures from left to right, as though you were looking at them face-on. As you do so, insert a number from 1 to 13 in the spaces next to the names of the figures, with 1 indicating the figure at the far left of the pediment and 13 the figure at the far right.

Continued overleaf

- The figures at the far left and far right represent Uncivilized and Civilized Man, respectively

- Drama is the only figure separating Poetry and Mathematics

- The Farmer is shown to the immediate right of the Hunter

- The Angel is shown to the left of the figure representing Architecture, but not the immediate left

- Sculpture is shown to the immediate left of Painting, and both are to the left of Mathematics

- Mathematics and Science are next to each another

- Music is shown immediately to the right of Poetry

- Architecture is shown to the immediate right of the Farmer

- The Angel is shown immediately next to Uncivilized Man – leading him from the wild with a golden lamp

- Sculpture is not the third figure from the left

.... ANGEL   .... MATHEMATICS

.... ARCHITECTURE   .... MUSIC

.... CIVILIZED MAN   .... PAINTING

.... DRAMA   .... POETRY

.... FARMER   .... SCIENCE

.... HUNTER   .... SCULPTURE

                                         .... UNCIVILIZED MAN

Continued from previous page

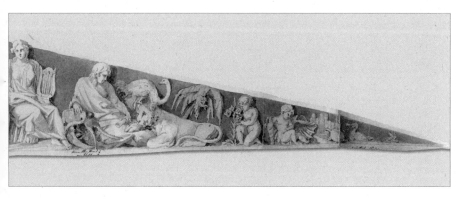

Details from Sir Richard Westmacott's original design for the sculptures in the pediment of the portico of the British Museum.

2. Glass Ceiling

The glass roof that covers the British Museum's Great Court, a section of which is shown below, is both a thing of beauty and a staggering feat of engineering. Composed of triangular panels of glass, the roof created the largest covered public square in Europe when it was completed in 2000. Incredibly, and despite appearances to the contrary, no two glass panels are exactly the same.

Piece together the triangular panels opposite, placing them in the empty framework provided so that one number is revealed in each of the first two rows and three numbers in the bottom row. None of the pieces needs rotating. When the pieces are correctly placed, the numbers pointed to by each labelled arrow will reveal the following:

A = total weight of the glass panels, in tonnes
B = number of individual panels that make up the roof
C = size of the inner courtyard in acres
D = greatest height of the roof in metres
E = number of weeks needed to clean the roof

DID YOU KNOW ...?

The glass panels are not motionless: thanks to a type of technology known as 'sliding bearings', the panels can expand and contract in response to changes in the weather and climate, such as snow or extreme heat.

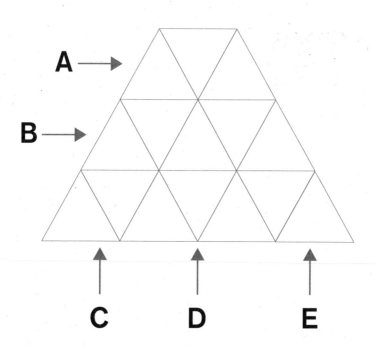

3. Reading Maze

The British Museum's Reading Room has welcomed many eminent guests during its lifetime. Former visitors include the writers Sir Arthur Conan Doyle, Bram Stoker and Virginia Woolf; even Vladimir Lenin paid a visit, signing in with a pseudonym. The room was a sensation when it first opened, an event marked by a special, one-off public viewing attended by more than 62,000 people.

Explore the room yourself by finding a path from the entrance at the top of the circular maze, opposite, to the exit at the bottom, without retracing your steps. Your route will pass over several digits. When these digits are read in order from entrance to exit, the resulting number will give you the date on which the Reading Room was officially opened, in DD/MM/YYYY format.

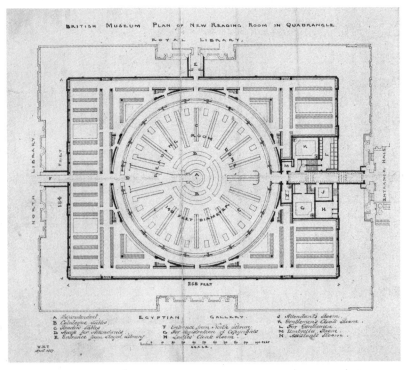

The earliest existing plan of the Reading Room.

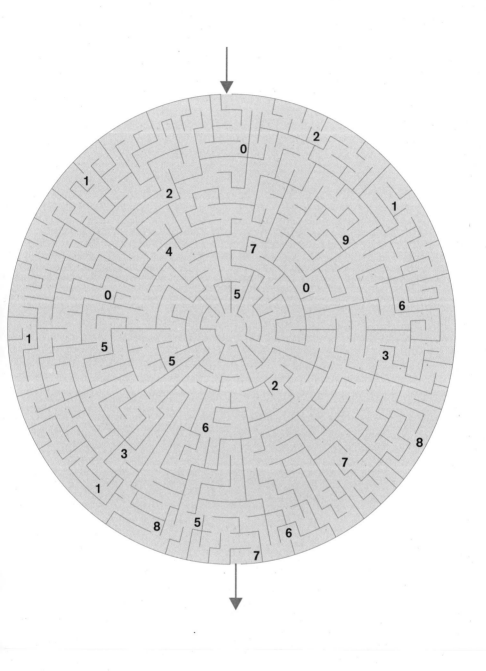

The Reading Room was officially opened on _____ / _____ / _____

4. Match the '-ology'

Below are the names of six areas of study, while opposite are six artefacts from the British Museum.

Can you match each area of study with the artefact it applies to?

Area of study: Artefact:

1.   Conchology   _____

2.   Vexillology   _____

3.   Deltiology   _____

4.   Campanology   _____

5.   Oology   _____

6.   Balneology   _____

A.

B.

C.

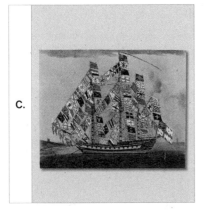

D.

E.

F.

5. An Unusual Discovery

The sarcophagus shown below is of Romano-British origin, made in the 4th century CE. When curators at the British Museum opened it up, however, they found an unusual item inside, thought to have been left there by a previous curator who had first examined the coffin long before.

The item, whose name consists of one word, can be spelled out using all of the letters in the circle below exactly once. What anachronistic item was found inside? Write your answer on the line at the bottom of the page.

Additionally, the names of the objects pictured below – or one of their principal features – can also be spelled out using the letters in the circle. Each name uses the central letter plus two or more of the other letters, with no letter being used more times than it appears in the circle. Can you find and write in the relevant words for each of the six objects?

A.

B.

C.

D.

E.

F.

Finally, more than a hundred additional words can be found using the central letter plus two or more of the other letters, without using any letter more times than it appears. How many can you find?

6. Cats' Tales

Until the 1990s, the British Museum was home to several cats, which were kept for their mouse- and rat-catching skills. Perhaps the most famous was Mike, a tabby who guarded the gates of the museum and was particularly known for chasing dogs away.

Solve the sudoku-style puzzle below to reveal the two-word name of the cat who first brought Mike into the British Museum as a kitten, dropping him at the feet of the Keeper of Egyptian Antiquities. To do so, place one of the letters A, B, C, E, J, K, L, S or T into each empty square, so that no letter repeats in any row, column or bold-lined 3×3 box. Once you've completed the puzzle, the letters in the shaded diagonal will reveal – when read from top left to bottom right – the name of Mike's feline friend.

				C				
		E	K	J	A	C		
	S		L		E		T	
	B	S				J	A	
J	E						L	C
	C	L				T	K	
	K		B		C		S	
		B	J	T	K	E		
				A				

MIKE
THE
BRITISH MUSEUM CAT
1909 – 1929
A JUBILEE REMINISCENCE

1979
BLOOMSBURY

The cover of a pamphlet about Mike the cat, published on the 50th anniversary of his death.

Mike, the tabby cat of the British Museum, who has just celebrated his fourteenth birthday, has an honourable record as a law officer against thieves who break in and nibble.

An extract from a pamphlet published by the British Museum in 1929 to mark Mike's passing.

7. Rainbow Railings

Although they might look as though they have been painted black, the railings around the British Museum are in fact coated in a very unusual colour. The name of the colour has two parts: an initial adjective followed by a more familiar colour name.

Listed below are several adjectives and colours that, when combined, could make up the name of the paint used for the railings. All of these words can be found in the grid opposite, except for two. Words may be written in any direction in a straight line, including backwards or diagonally. The two words that *cannot* be found in the grid, when read in the order 'ADJECTIVE COLOUR', will reveal the name of the unusual paint.

Adjectives	Colours
CLANDESTINE	BLACK
CONCEALED	BLUE
COVERT	BROWN
DISGUISED	CRIMSON
FURTIVE	GREEN
HIDDEN	INDIGO
INVISIBLE	NAVY
MYSTERIOUS	ORANGE
PRIVATE	PINK
SECRET	RED
STEALTHY	VIOLET
UNDERCOVER	WHITE
UNKNOWN	YELLOW
UNSEEN	

```
Y H T L A E T S X J E K Y G H
C L A N D E S T I N E V B B Y
Y N V W H I T E M N A B L U E
E G O R L F B G M N D A Q T X
L D I S G U I S E D C I I B E
L F E W M X J Q N K G U G R T
O U K D C I A T Q W G K N O A
W R Y E E K R J R K O E O W V
S T A R E V O C R E D N U N I
E I L N E E S N U D V X K Z R
C V Z V G M Z Y I E M O O N P
R E V F K E P H P I J K C L U
E X E R N M Y S T E R I O U S
T E L O I V C O N C E A L E D
R R P R P K F R H X W A P O S
```

Unusual paint colour:

_____   _____

8. Discus: Discuss

This marble statue of a nude discus-thrower, displayed in the British Museum, is one of many surviving copies of a lost bronze original. Yet it stands out from the crowd of copies owing to an unusual flaw. Can you work out what that flaw is?

Listed below are the Greek names of some of the events that made up the Ancient Olympic Games, including the one being demonstrated opposite. However, each of these words has had the same simple change applied to it, which, in turn, hints at the unique flaw exhibited by the discus-thrower statue. English descriptions of each event are also provided, for reference.

What do you think is wrong with the statue?

Greek name	Description
HALMA	long jump
2TADE	≈190m sprint
ᗡIAULOS	≈400m sprint
ᗡOLICHOS	≈4800m run
2YNORIS	2-horse chariot race
ꟼALE	wrestling
ꟼYGME	boxing
ꓘELES	horse race
ᗡISKOS	discus

9. True or False?

In addition to documenting millions of years of history through its collections, the British Museum as a building – and as an institution – has its own unique tales to tell.

Half of these statements about the Museum are true and half are false. Using your knowledge and judgment, try to work out which is which.

1.   The British Museum and the United States of America were founded in the same year. ☐

2.   The British Museum introduced electric lighting in 1879. ☐

3.   A snail, glued to a card and exhibited in the British Museum, was found to be alive after four years of being on display. ☐

4.   'Marbles' is the most searched-for term on the British Museum website. ☐

5.   During both world wars, the British Museum evacuated some of its artefacts and exhibitions to Wales, in case of attack. ☐

6.   The street artist Banksy spray-painted an image of a mouse on to a Museum wall in 2005. ☐

7.   The British Museum once had its own London Underground station. ☐

8.   The film *Vertigo*, directed by Alfred Hitchcock, was partly filmed at the British Museum. ☐

9.   A young W. A. Mozart visited the British Museum on an outing with his family shortly after it opened. ☐

10. The main entrance to the British Museum is on Bloomsbury Street, London. ☐

2

Everyday Living

Exploring 2 million years of human history highlights the similarities and differences between how we live today and the practices of our earliest ancestors. Objects from the Museum's collection illustrate the daily lives of ancient peoples, who shared our most significant as well as our most trivial concerns. From Pharaonic decrees inscribed in stone to shopping lists scribbled on Roman tablets, from exquisite banqueting tableware to single-use disposable cups, and from colossal sculpture to pin badges, the vast collection allows the curious to discover the many facets of human history and culture.

1. The Cities that Were

These tombstones were made in Britain in the 1st century CE, when much of England was under Roman rule. Both stones are dedicated to military men who were buried in the same Roman city, located somewhere in Britain. To find out where, and the modern-day city to which this and four other Roman settlements correspond, complete the puzzle opposite. The tombstones come from city number 3.

First, use your knowledge of British geography to identify the names of the modern locations from the given clues, entering one letter per box in each top row. Then, copy the linked letters to the connected boxes on the bottom row. Once complete, each bottom row will spell out the equivalent Roman name of that place.

1. England's capital

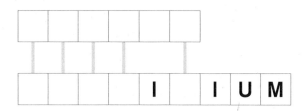

2. Port town in south-east England

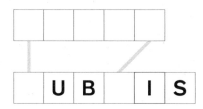

3. Cathedral city south of the River Humber

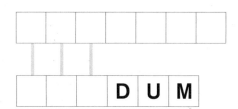

4. Cumbrian city near Hadrian's Wall

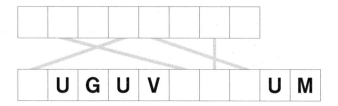

5. Cathedral city on the River Severn

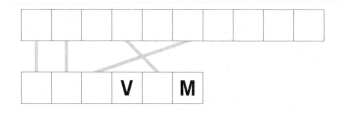

2. Fun and Games

Evidence of the playing of board games can be found throughout human history, dating back to at least 5,000 years ago. The games themselves typically involved a board with movable playing pieces, and have been found in widely varying cultures across the world. Some of these ancient games are still known and played today, such as backgammon, while others have fallen out of favour over the years.

Solve the clues opposite to uncover the names of several antique pastimes that can be found on display in the British Museum. The numbers in brackets indicate the length of each clued word, and all of the solution names can be found, in clue order, in the letter grid below. Trace out a path that visits each square once, moving horizontally or vertically between letters while spelling out the names. Your path should begin on the white (blank) square and end on the shaded one.

Once you have found all nine names, try to match each game to its corresponding image on page 32.

	C	M	E	H	C	H
E	H	I	R	E	A	I
S	E	N	A	N	P	S
S	S	E	W	G	N	I
O	G	T	D	I	O	U
R	U	S	E	C	J	R
O	K	U	M	A	H	

Name: Image:

1. Played on a board with 64 squares, the Western version of this strategic game emerged in Spain around the 15th century (5)

2. Although the rules of this two-player game from ancient Egypt have since been lost, some versions are thought to have represented the soul's journey to the afterlife (5)

3. A general name for games played with usually cubic pieces whose sides are marked with dots to each indicate a different number (4)

4. This Japanese word originally referred to a game somewhat like backgammon, but which was later simplified to play more like snakes and ladders (8)

5. This game has a name that in some Chinese languages means 'sparrow' – a reference to the sound made during the shuffling of the 144 tiles used in play (7)

6. This is one of various names given to the many variations of this 'pit and pebble' strategy game, whose origins lie in Africa (4)

7. This ancient Egyptian game is named after the snake deity represented by the spiral, chequered board on which it is played (5)

8. This ancient Indian game is played with cowrie shells and a cross-shaped board, and has a name derived from the Hindi word for 'twenty-five' – the highest score possible in a single turn (7)

9. This two-player racing game from ancient Mesopotamia is the oldest still-playable board game in the world, thanks to the careful deciphering of its cuneiform rule book (2)

Continued overleaf →

A.

B.

C.

D.

E.

F.

G.

H.

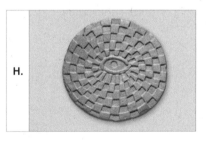

I.

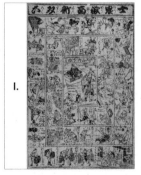

Continued from previous page

3. The Lewis Chessmen

Discovered in 1831 on a Scottish island, the Lewis Chessmen are a large collection of chess pieces thought to have been made in the 12th century. With six kings, five queens, thirteen bishops, fourteen knights, ten rooks and nineteen pawns in the collection of the British Museum, it's clear that the pieces came from multiple chess sets.

Solve the crossword clues overleaf, completing the puzzle in the usual way, to reveal some further facts about these legendary figures. When complete, the letters in the shaded squares can be rearranged to spell out the two-word name of a well-known film series in which animated versions of the Lewis Chessmen appear.

A selection of the 78 pieces that make up the Lewis Chessmen.

 Continued overleaf

Across

4. Scottish archipelagos, can be Inner or Outer (8)
7. Chess piece (4)
8. Protective armour depicted on some pieces (6)
10. Archaic chess piece; custodian (6)
12. Standard colour of some chess pieces (5)
13. Shape of 7 across, in the Lewis sets (7)
15. Mammal whose teeth were used to make some pieces (5)
18. Scottish bay where the pieces were found (3)
19. Material used to make several pieces (5)
20. Marine mammal whose tusks provide 19 across (6)
21. Chess piece (6)

Down

1. Chess piece (5)
2. Scandinavian country, thought to be the sets' origin (6)
3. Frenzied Viking warrior, from which we derive a word for 'crazed' (9)
5. Weapon depicted on some pieces (5)
6. Colour shown on some Lewis pieces (3)
9. Chess piece (6)
11. Scottish city where some pieces are kept (9)
14. Chess piece (4)
16. Scottish island where the pieces were found (5)
17. Chess piece (4)

DID YOU KNOW ...?

The Lewis Chessmen are some of the most widely travelled and exhibited objects in the British Museum's collection, with various pieces shown in more than twenty exhibitions around the world since 1995.

Continued from previous page

Film series:

_____ _____

4. Everyday A-maze-ing

Today, Greek pottery is perhaps better known for its artwork than for its functionality, but vases, amphorae and kraters were designed for everyday use. Geometric motifs began to appear from around 1000 BCE and the trend continued for centuries, eventually resulting in the kind of labyrinthine patterns that can be seen on the pottery items illustrated below.

In a similarly labyrinthine experience, try to find your way from the entrance at the top of the maze opposite to its exit without retracing your path. Your route will then pass over six numbers, which you should write out in the order of encounter to create a six-digit number. This figure represents the total number of Greek artefacts held by the British Museum, as of the date of writing.

The patterns on this amphora (left) and pitcher (right) have been attributed to the Dipylon Painter or his workshop, active between 760 and 750 BCE.

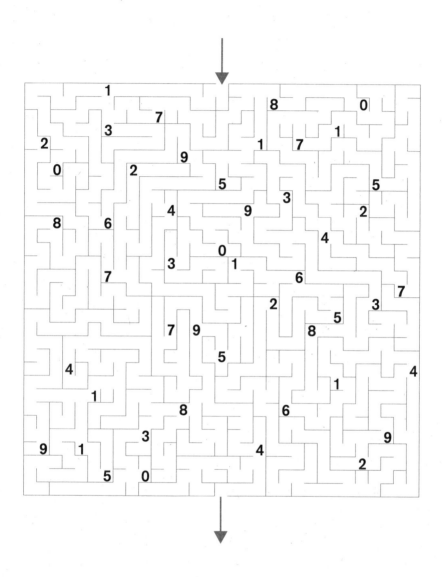

Write the six-digit number here:

— — — — — —

5. Undiluted Beauty

The basin shown opposite, pictured on its stand, was used in ancient Greece for diluting wine. The item is adorned with images of a mythical wedding (see detail, below), in which each of the divine attendees has been helpfully labelled by the artist. The basin, or *dinos*, also carries an inscription that, when translated into English, identifies the painter by name – making them the earliest Greek painter whose name is definitively known.

Place each of the gods listed below into one of the horizontal rows opposite, one letter per box, so that an English translation of the artist's inscription is revealed in the grey squares when read from top to bottom. Some letters have been given to help you get started.

AMPHITRITE
APHRODITE
APOLLO
ARES
ARTEMIS
ATHENA
CHIRON
DIONYSUS
FATES

HEBE
HEPHAISTOS
HERA
PELEUS
POSEIDON
TETHYS
THETIS
ZEUS

This *dinos* was produced in the late 6th century BCE. A detail of its decoration is shown opposite.

6. Complaining for Ages

**The cuneiform tablet shown below is thought to be the world's
oldest written customer complaint, created in 1750 BCE by
someone known as Nanni. Their chief concern appears to
have been the poor quality of some metal goods.**

In the abridged transcription of the complaint opposite, the words
in capital letters are deliberately misspelled English translations in
which there is exactly one incorrect letter. Can you therefore change
one letter in each of the uppercase words to reveal the correct
contents of Nanni's complaint?

'When you came, you said to me as follows: "I will give Gimil-Sin (when he COMBS) FIND quality COPIER ingots." You LENT then but you did not do what you PREMISED me. You CUT ingots that were not GOLD before my messenger (Sit-Sin) and PAID: "If you want to MAKE them, TAME them; if you do not want to WAKE them, go away!" What do you FAKE me for, that you GREAT somebody like me with MUCH contempt … Take cognisance that (from NEW on) I will not ACCENT here any COPTER from you that is not of FIRE quality. I shall (from NOT on) select and BAKE the ingots individually in my own YARN, and I SMALL exercise against you my MIGHT of DEJECTION because you have CREATED me with contempt.'

7. Keeping Track

The hinged brass calendar whose front and back are shown below was made in Germany in the 1600s. Inscribed on one side of the calendar are the names of several animals hunted in the medieval period, along with illustrations.

The names of five of these animals are hidden in the explanatory text opposite, one per sentence. For example, 'DOG' is hidden in 'Not all hunters <u>do g</u>ood deeds'. Each of the animal names is exactly four letters long. Are you able to hunt them all down?

- The calendar was designed for riders to inscribe a record of their hunts over the course of a year

Animal: _____

- Red wax strips provide erasable – and reusable – areas for marking the time and date of successful pursuits

Animal: _____

- The German names for each month are shown on the right-hand side of the calendar, as can be seen in the lower image opposite

Animal: _____

- Hunting dogs of different breeds, each noted for their accurate, narrow olfaction, are also illustrated

Animal: _____

- Medieval hunters may have travelled long distances in pursuit of their quarry, staying with local families and landed gentry

Animal: _____

DID YOU KNOW ...?

Hunting calendars such as these were also engraved with detailed information about the times of the sun's rising and setting, as well as the exact length of day and night for each week.

8. Cups and Saucers

While the cup and saucer might seem like an indivisible pairing today, that has not always been the case. Tea and coffee were both initially drunk from bowls without handles – like two of the examples shown opposite – before the spread of these hot drinks and their culture to the West, where handles and saucers were added.

The grid below is partially filled with cups (in white) and saucers (in grey). Can you mimic the spread of cups and saucers across the world by drawing more cups and saucers, placing one in every currently empty square? They must be placed so that no lines of four or more of the same item are formed in any direction, including diagonally, anywhere in the grid.

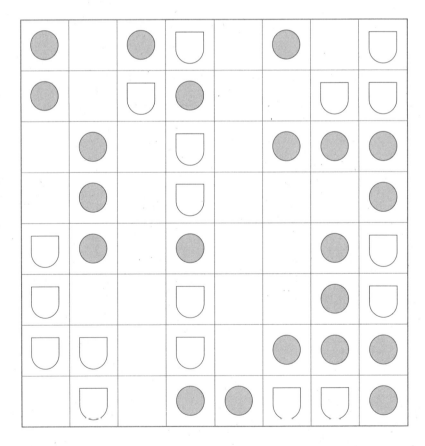

From top: a miniature cup and saucer made in
Staffordshire in the 18th century; a tea-bowl from
16th-century Japan; a Japanese cup and saucer
from the early 18th century; a late 17th-century
coffee cup made in Iran.

9. Hadrian's Wall

The Roman emperor Hadrian is perhaps best known for the wall
he commissioned in the north of England that now bears his name.
Hadrian's wall stretched almost from coast to coast, separating
Roman-ruled Britannia from the unconquered Caledonia to the north.

Create your own dividing wall in the grid below, splitting the grid into
two separate areas – one to the north of the wall (i.e. above it), and
one to the south of the wall (i.e. below it). To do so, draw a wall from
'Bowness-on-Solway' on the left to 'Wallsend' on the right. Numbers
outside the grid reveal the exact number of squares in each row and
column that contain a part of the wall. Every wall piece must either
go straight through or turn a right-angled corner in a square, and the
wall cannot cross over itself or have any 'dead ends'.

When complete, count how many grid squares your wall passes through
to reveal the approximate age at which Hadrian is depicted in this
bronze bust.

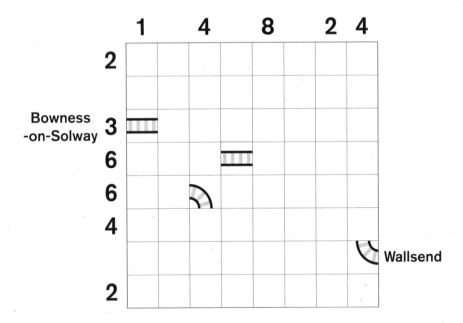

Approximate age of Hadrian: _____

Found in the River Thames, this rare bronze bust of Hadrian comes from a statue of the emperor that probably stood in one of Roman London's public spaces.

10. Glass Fragments

Mosaic glass, as can be seen from the bowls shown below, is made by 'slicing' cylindrical canes of decorative glass into pieces, and then fusing together the slices to create a jigsaw-like design. Many of the examples in the British Museum were made in the Hellenistic period, beginning around 300 BCE – and, as such, many of them show signs of breakage and fragmentation.

In this puzzle, you must restore some glass by placing the geometric fragments shown at the top of the opposite page into the framework below them, in such a way that two words can be read in each line of resulting text. Three pieces have been placed already to get you started. When read in order from top to bottom, the completed message will name a glass-related project initiated by the British Museum in 2020.

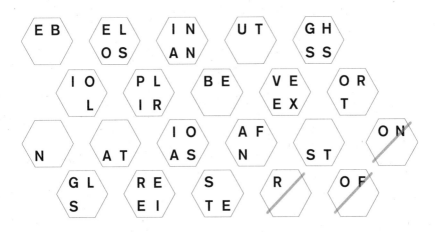

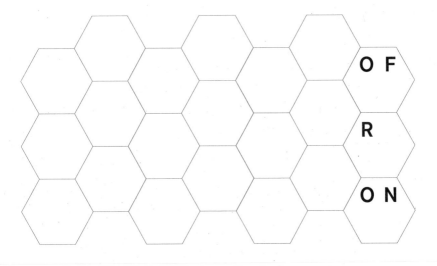

11. Finding the Way

The cane and shell navigation charts shown below were made in the Marshall Islands, located in the centre of the Pacific Ocean, and were used to plot the locations of known island chains. Other similar charts were used to mark out typical patterns of waves and swells around hypothetical islands, to help seafarers learn the habits of the sea.

Create your own navigation chart in the square opposite, joining islands (the circled numbers) to one another with horizontal or vertical lines, but never diagonally. There can be zero, one or two lines between any given pair of islands, but lines cannot cross over one another or pass through an island. There must be as many connecting lines attached to each island as indicated by the number printed on it. The finished layout must also be designed in such a way that it connects all of the islands, thereby allowing you to travel between any pair of islands by following one or more lines.

Ignore the letters while solving the puzzle. Once you have completed it, however, read all of the letters that have been crossed by lines, in order from left to right and top to bottom, to reveal the name given to these navigational charts.

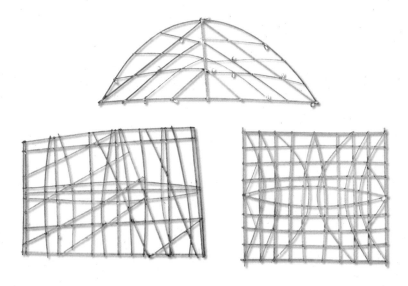

(2) R (3) (4) (6) (3)

(1) (2) E (1) A (1) (2) (1)

(4) (3) (1) B (3) (1)

B (3) (2) (4) (4)

S (3) (4) K E

F (3) I (4) (3)

(3) (2) C T

(5) (5) (2) (5) (2)

E (3) (4) (4) (3)

(1) L (3) (5) (2)

O (1) M (1)

(4) (2) (3) (3)

(1) I (3) (4) B (5) (4) (2)

Chart name: _____

12. Loop the Loop

The Roman sock pictured below is thought to have been made as early as the 3rd century CE, using a technique known as nalbinding. The technique involves 'knitting' with a single needle, using several short threads that are then felted together to create an apparently continuous loop. When complete, the resulting garment cannot be unravelled.

In a similar vein, can you join up all the short threads in this puzzle square, to create a looped pattern that visits all of the dots? Specifically, join all of the dots in a single loop that does not cross or touch itself at any point, using only horizontal and vertical lines.

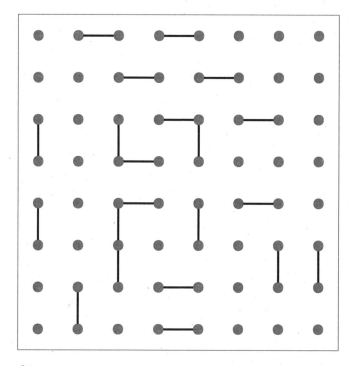

13. Musical Marvel

The artefact shown at the bottom of this page is a citole – a lute-like instrument associated with medieval ballads and love songs. As well as the intricate wooden carving depicting scenes of nature and hunting, this example features a silver plaque engraved with the coat of arms of an English noble – a person for whom this particular citole may have been significant.

The name of the person has been encoded below, disguised as a kind of musical notation. If the first row of notes represents 'CITOLE', then what name is represented by the row beneath it?

The featured coat of arms belonged to:

_____

14. A Load of Old Rubbish

Pictured below is a disposable cup made from clay, found in Crete. Several cups of this type were found together in the Palace of Knossos, indicating that they may have been made hastily for an event and discarded afterwards. Much like a modern disposable plastic cup, it has a lifespan measured in centuries once discarded, although the environmental impact of clay cups is relatively minimal in terms of harmful contamination.

More disposable cups have been hidden in the grid opposite, and can be revealed by using the number clues. Each clue indicates the total number of cups buried in its surrounding touching squares – including the squares that touch it diagonally. No more than one cup can be found in any square, and there are none in the squares with numbers. Can you find all the cups? Once you have finished locating them, count the number of cups and multiply that number by 100 to reveal the approximate year BCE in which the cup shown below was made.

2	3	4		2	2	
				3		
3		6	4			2
	2				1	
1			3			
				2		2
1	2	1			3	

Approximate year the cup was made:

_____

15. Age-Old Eats

Surprisingly, exhibits at the British Museum include food products, some of which are thousands of years old.

The names of several foods on display at the Museum are given below, although they have been broken up and the resulting pieces placed in alphabetical order. Rearrange the pieces to restore the single-word names of the foods, and then match each resulting word to one of the images shown opposite.

AD	BRE	CK	CO
DU	F	FI	IE
IGS	OK	PA	RY
	SH	ST	

When the restored food products are listed in alphabetical order, the first one in the list will be an anagram of the surname of a renowned classical historian and contemporary trustee of the British Museum. The historian, in turn, was previously inspired by this very food product on a visit to the British Museum aged five. Who is it, and which food artefact inspired them?

Historian:　　　　　　　　　　　　Food artefact:

_____　　_____

A.

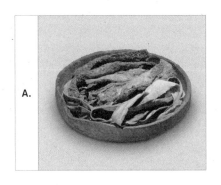

Food: _____

B.

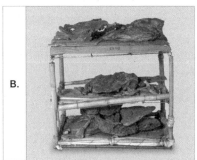

Food: _____

C.

Food: _____

D.

Food: _____

E.

Food: _____

F.

Food: _____

The Animal Kingdom

Wild and wonderful depictions of animals can be found throughout the Museum's collection. Whether it be the monumental stone sculptures of human–animal hybrids that originally guarded the entrance to the throne room of King Ashurnasirpal II at Nimrud in modern-day Iraq, medieval depictions of unicorns and centaurs, the exquisitely carved Japanese netsuke of a tiny rat, or Beatrix Potter's captivating world of the Flopsy Bunnies, all ages and cultures have created images of animals, both real and imagined.

1. Colossal Animals

The collection of the British Museum includes several colossal statues of animals, some almost three metres long.

Each image at the bottom of this page shows just part of one of these statues, while each frame below shows only part of a letter from an animal's name, with one animal per line. Are you able to identify the animals from their partial letters, and then match each animal name with one of the partial views of a giant statue?

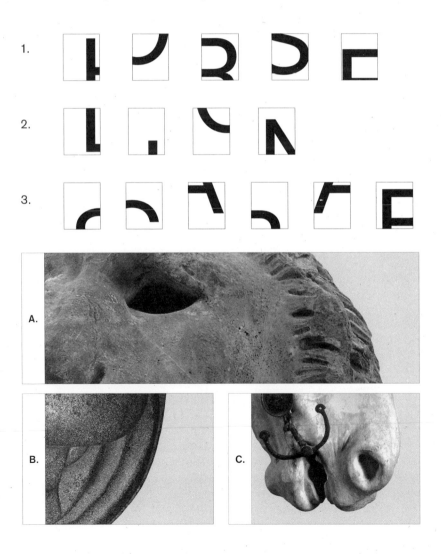

2. Immortal Animals 1

These animals have been immortalized as sculptures, each made from a different material.

For each line below, separate the name of an animal from the material it was sculpted from, and then match it to one of the seven images opposite. The letters for each animal and material have been mixed together, but remain in the correct order – for example, PMIGUD would be PIG + MUD.

1. JOAWDLE

    Animal: _____ Material: _____ Image: _____

2. LBAIPRIDS

    Animal: _____ Material: _____ Image: _____

3. BRCONAZTE

    Animal: _____ Material: _____ Image: _____

4. GYLPISOUNM

    Animal: _____ Material: _____ Image: _____

5. PCLAMASETLER

    Animal: _____ Material: _____ Image: _____

6. NETEPRRHARPIITNE

    Animal: _____ Material: _____ Image: _____

7. THEIRPRPAOPCOOTATMTUAS

    Animal: _____ Material: _____ Image: _____

A.

B.

C.

D.

E.

G.

F.

3. Encoded Animals

Each of the four lists on this spread contains the names of the same eight animals, all of which can be found within ancient Egyptian hieroglyphs. The names of these animals, however, have been encoded in four different ways, with a different type of encoding used for each list. What's more, the encoded names are in a different order in each list.

Try to work out which eight animals have been encoded in each of the four different lists. To make things trickier, an additional secret word has been added to each list, encoded according to that list's rules. When these four secret words are deciphered, they will spell out a secret message. What is it?

List 1:

DPCSB

HFDLP

JCFY

JCJT

KBDLBM

PQFO

PSZY

UJMBQJB

WVMUVSF

List 2:

10-1-3-11-1-12

15-18-25-24

20-8-5

20-9-12-1-16-9-1

22-21-12-20-21-18-5

3-15-2-18-1

7-5-3-11-15

9-2-5-24

9-2-9-19

A 'Book of the Dead' papyrus from the 19th Dynasty of Egypt (1292 to 1189 BCE)

List 3:

AJKCLA

BISI

BIXE

EGKCO

ITALIPA

OCRBA

OTBM

ROXY

UVTLRUE

List 4:

CUBRE

GICKU

JECKEL

OBIX

OBOS

QAOITLY

TOLEPOE

URYX

VALTARI

4. In the Labyrinth

Cultures throughout the world have incorporated mythical creatures into their folklore, passing them down through the ages in their storytelling traditions and art.

Trace your way through this labyrinth of letters by moving just one square at a time, spelling out the names of seven mythical creatures as you go. Your path can only move horizontally or vertically between touching squares, and cannot revisit any square.

Start your adventure at the arrow on the outer edge of the labyrinth and travel all the way to the shaded square at the centre, having visited every square. What is the final creature you encounter before you make it to the centre of the labyrinth?

Mythical creatures:

A	I	D	P	H	O
M	M	N	I	S	X	E
E	R	X	H	P	I	N
R	I	S		A	T	O
E	N	G	R	U	I	N
F	I	R	N	I	M	N
F	I	N	U	C	O	R

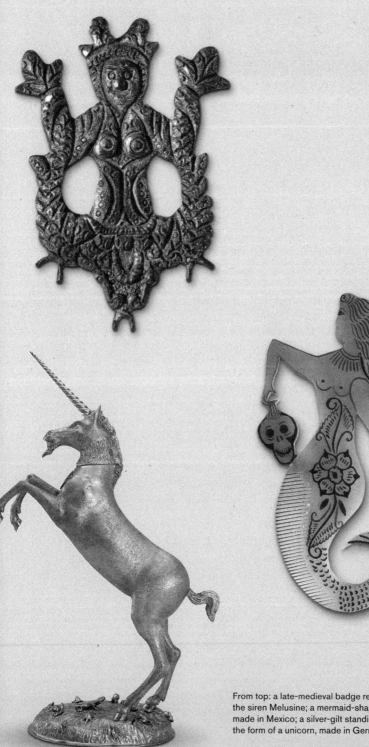

From top: a late-medieval badge representing
the siren Melusine; a mermaid-shaped comb
made in Mexico; a silver-gilt standing cup in
the form of a unicorn, made in Germany.

5. Sacred Animal Pairs

Many deities from Greek mythology are closely associated with elements of the natural world, especially flora and fauna.

On each line below, the name of a Greek god or goddess has been paired with an animal whose name contains the same number of letters as the name of the god or goddess and which is sacred to that deity. The letters of both names have then been grouped into pairs, with each pair taking one letter from the name of the deity and one from that of the animal, with all letters remaining in the correct order for each word. For example, HERA and CALF might have been written as CH AE LR AF.

Can you separate the pairs of letters to reveal the gods or goddesses and their sacred animals, and then match each of these animals to one of the pictured artefacts?

1. **BZ EU LU SL**

    Deity: _____   Animal: _____   Artefact: _____

2. **CA PI CO AL DL OA**

    Deity: _____   Animal: _____   Artefact: _____

3. **BA OR EA RS**

    Deity: _____   Animal: _____   Artefact: _____

4. **SD EE RM PE ET EN TR**

    Deity: _____   Animal: _____   Artefact: _____

5. **HD OE NS TK EI AY**

    Deity: _____   Animal: _____   Artefact: _____

6. **LR HI OE AN**

    Deity: _____   Animal: _____   Artefact: _____

A.

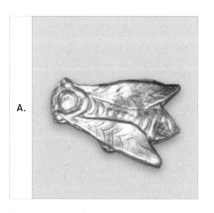

B.

C.

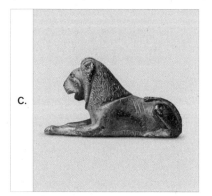

D.

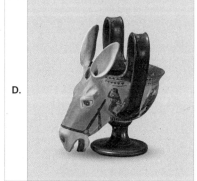

E.

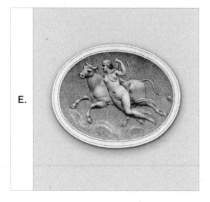

F.

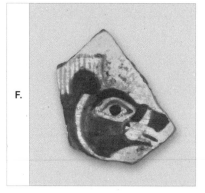

6. Hunting the Hunted

Eight animals that were once (or still are) hunted are hiding in the word-search grid opposite.

They are so well camouflaged, however, that only their initial letter and the total number of letters in their names are given in the list of words to find. Can you identify all eight animals and then locate them in the grid, written in any direction?

All but one of these animals can also be found on 'The Hunters' Palette', shown below. Are you able to work out which animal is not pictured?

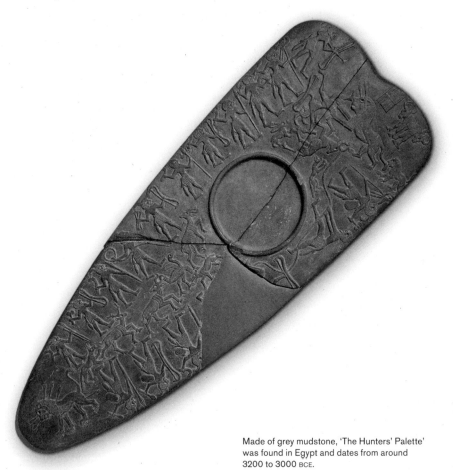

Made of grey mudstone, 'The Hunters' Palette' was found in Egypt and dates from around 3200 to 3000 BCE.

```
Z K I E A S R E E D L R H
E Z H R H I A C R A T A N
N E R A R R S A S A R H B
O G R K D T R H L T I I A
S E E S B S A R E N E B O
T H O L R A B B Z C R O E
R T R T L E E R R A R A A
I T R C I E B A C O E R G
C Z T H S S Z E A A R E T
H I C T C L G A A R R L A
B E I C A L Z B G J I H A
J A C K A L A O I O Z A C
R A L R R R L H N L K E I
```

4 letters:

B _ _ _

D _ _ _

H _ _ _

L _ _ _

6 letters:

J _ _ _ _ _

7 letters:

G _ _ _ _ _ _

O _ _ _ _ _ _

10 letters:

H _ _ _ _ _ _ _ _ _

7. Therianthropic Theory

Although visual representations of Egyptian gods have varied by era, many of the well-known deities are consistently portrayed as having the bodies or heads of animals.

Using the text below, pair each of the Egyptian gods on the left with the name of the animal whose head they are often depicted as having on the right, drawing a straight line that joins their associated dots. Once correctly drawn, the six lines will pass through six letters (one per line) and spell out from top to bottom the name of a well-known animal-headed god from Hindu mythology. What is that god's name, and can you say which animal head they have?

God: _____ Animal head: _____

Anubis •   M   A   G   • Crocodile
                        L
Horus •   A   E   • Ram
                        I
                            N
Sobek •   U   O   • Lioness
                        S   E
                    C B
Amun •   X   • Falcon
                    H   S   P
Thoth •   R   • Jackal
                    H   J
Sekhmet •   Y   T   • Ibis

A selection of small statues depicting
four different ancient Egyptian gods.

8. Immortal Animals 2

These animals have been immortalized as sculptures, each made from a different material.

For each line below, separate the name of an animal from the material it was sculpted from, and then match it to one of the seven images opposite. The letters for each animal and material have been mixed together, but remain in the correct order – for example, PMIGUD would be PIG + MUD.

1. DCLOGAY

    Animal: _____ Material: _____ Image: _____

2. CBOUPPLERL

    Animal: _____ Material: _____ Image: _____

3. CIARTFOINSH

    Animal: _____ Material: _____ Image: _____

4. CACLOCIWTE

    Animal: _____ Material: _____ Image: _____

5. TMAIRGBELRE

    Animal: _____ Material: _____ Image: _____

6. STUTROTNELE

    Animal: _____ Material: _____ Image: _____

7. TBORUTOTITSEERSHFELYLL

    Animal: _____ Material: _____ Image: _____

9. Start and End

The fantastical creatures shown opposite both have two heads
– one at each end of their bodies.

The animals below also have identical heads and tails, but only their
names have this property; EWE and TROUT, for example, both start
and end with the same letter. Can you work out which animals are
depicted in the boxes? The number of letters in each of their names
has been given. The six first-and-last letters are: A, D, E, G, R and R.

A.

9 letters

B.

7 letters

C.

6 letters

D.

9 letters

E.

5 letters

F.

8 letters

A double-headed serpent from the Aztec period. Made of cedro wood covered with tiny fragments of oyster shell, the object is thought to represent a 'sky-band', symbolizing the celestial realm.

This carved wooden figure of a two-headed dog is attributed to Kongo people of the west coast of Central Africa, who regard domesticated animals, such as dogs, as mediators between the worlds of the living and the dead.

10. The Four Sons of Horus

In Egyptian mythology, the Four Sons of the god Horus are each depicted with the head of a different creature.

Use the following clues to assign the correct name to the four amulets shown opposite, which each represent one of the Four Sons.

- The four sons are: Duamutef, Hapy, Imsety and Qebehsenuef

- The protector of intestines is shown with the head of a falcon

- Imsety is not the figure with a jackal's head

- Hapy was not considered the protector of the stomach or liver

- Duamutef is not the figure with the baboon's head

- The figure with a human head was traditionally the protector of the liver

- Qebehsenuef is the protector of the intestines

- The baboon-headed figure is said to be a protector of the lungs

DID YOU KNOW ...?

The ancient Egyptian god Horus is usually depicted as a falcon, his right eye taking the form of the sun or morning star, representing power and quintessence, and his left eye taking the form of the moon or evening star, representing healing.

From left to right, the four amulets depict:

_____

_____

_____

_____

11. Cat Caption Competition

Sacred to the Egyptians and often associated with luck – both good and bad – cats have featured in art and culture from across the globe for thousands of years.

Each of the four works of cat-centric art shown opposite has had every other letter removed from its title. Try to restore the missing letters to reveal the English names of the pieces, and then match each title to its corresponding image.

Image:

1. T _ E _ _ A _ G _ _ C _ T   ____

2. _ L _ C _ A _ D _ H _ C _ E _ H _ R _ C _ T ____

3. C _ T _ O _ K _ N _ A _ R _ C _ F _ E _ D _

     N _ A _ _ S _ K _ S _   ____

4. H _ R _ I _ L _ E _ D O _ A _ _ O _ D _ I _ H   ____

DID YOU KNOW ...?

One of the oldest feline objects in the British Museum is the Gayer-Anderson cat, a bronze figure from ancient Egypt thought to have been made in around 600 BCE. The sculpture depicts the goddess Bastet, who often took the form of a cat-headed woman or lion.

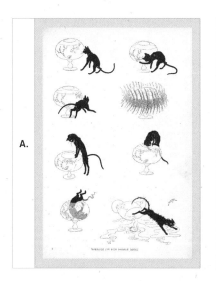

A.

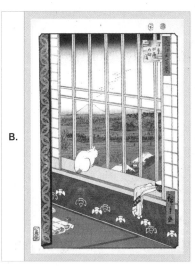

B.

C.

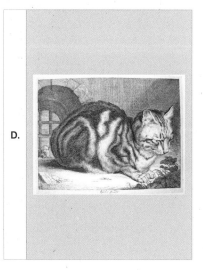

D.

12. Go Fish

The print shown below is an engraving made by Pieter van der Heyden in 1557. With accompanying text in both Flemish and Latin, it illustrates the Flemish proverb that forms its title: *Big Fish Eat Small Fish*.

Spend a few minutes studying the engraving. Once you think you have memorized the key details of the scene, turn the page and see how many of the questions you can answer without looking back at the engraving.

PISCES PISCIBVS ESCA.
dat die groote vissen de cleyne eten

Continued overleaf →

The questions below relate to the image on the previous page, *Big Fish Eat Small Fish*:

1. How many people are pictured in the large boat in the foreground of the image?

                _____

2. What is unusual about a fish shown on the land in the left-hand part of the image, just in front of the shed?

3. Which two crustaceans are shown walking towards the water in the centre of the image, below the big fish?

       _____   _____

4. How many fish are shown hanging from a tree in the background?

                _____

5. Which of these markings matches the one depicted on the knife used to cut open the big fish?

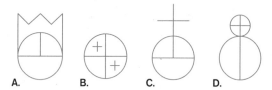

A.   B.   C.   D.

6. What Latin word, meaning 'look', is written as though it is being spoken by one of the figures in the boat?

       _____

Continued from previous page

13. What's in a Name?

With the world's oldest written joke thought to date from 1900 BCE, it is clear that humour has been a part of human culture since ancient times. These five Assyrian clay dogs, for example, are all inscribed with names that comically describe their fierce natures.

Unjumble the letters in each word below to reveal what these humorous names are. The punctuation and spaces have already been correctly placed.

YEMEN ARCHETC   _____

EYEMN TRIBE   _____

LUDO KRAREB   _____

EVERMOR FO LIVE   _____

NDO'T KNITH, ITBE   _____

14. Fishy Floor

The figures depicted in the intricate mosaic opposite – thought to have originally been part of the floor of a Roman dining room – are all edible creatures found in the Mediterranean Sea. Their names, however, have been broken up into many smaller pieces below.

Rearrange the pieces to reveal the creatures' names, using each fragment exactly once. The names should fit on to the given spaces below, with one letter per underline. The correct spacing for those creatures whose names consist of two words is already given.

ABA	AM	AS	AYE	BER	BRE
COM	DEN	EL	ENW	GRE	ISH
LET	MOR	MUL	NBO	NYL	OBS
OCT	ONF	OP	RAI	RAS	RPI
SCO	SE	SE	SE	SPI	SS
TER	TEX	US	WWR		

___ ___ ___ ___

___ ___ ___ ___ ___

___ ___ ___ ___

___ ___ ___ ___ ___

___ ___ ___ ___ ___   ___

___ ___ ___ ___ ___

___ ___ ___ ___   ___ ___ ___

___ ___ ___ ___ ___   ___ ___

___ ___ ___ ___ ___ ___   ___ ___ ___

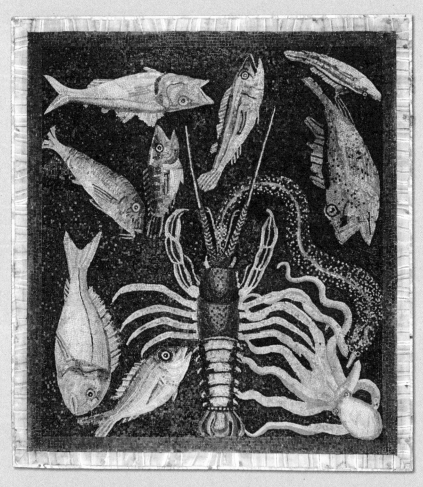

Panel from a mosaic floor, said to be from a house in
Populonia in north-west Italy. It dates from around 100 CE.

15. Animal Amulets

Various cultures throughout history have placed amulets on the bodies of the living and the dead, to help ensure protection and good fortune in this life and beyond.

Place each of the animals listed below – some of which are also depicted in amulet form – into the grid opposite, writing one letter per box so each word reads either across or down the page.

2 letter word
OX

3 letter words
APE
CAT
DOG
PIG
RAM

4 letter words
BULL
FISH
FROG
HARE
LION

5 letter words
HORSE
LLAMA
SHEEP

6 letter words
BABOON
FALCON

7 letter word
VULTURE

8 letter words
ANTELOPE
MONGOOSE

12 letter word
HIPPOPOTAMUS

A selection of amulets in animal form, from a dog with hooves from the 1st century BCE (above) to a dog-faced baboon from around 600 BCE.

16. Best Friends

Dogs have been depicted in painting and sculpture from ancient times to the modern day, marking an age-old relationship between humans and their four-legged friends.

All of the canine figures pictured opposite were made centuries apart in different places around the globe. Using your judgment, are you able to place the sculptures into chronological order of their creation by matching each image with one of the times and places below?

Sculpture:

- 2000–1700 BCE, Crete, Greece   _____

- 1350–1300 BCE, Thebes, Egypt   _____

- 600–580 BCE, Boeotia, Greece   _____

- 1st century BCE–2nd century CE, Egypt   _____

- 300 BCE–300 CE, Mexico   _____

- 150–50 BCE, Hounslow, England   _____

- 1st or 2nd century CE, China   _____

- 1st or 2nd century CE, Italy   _____

A.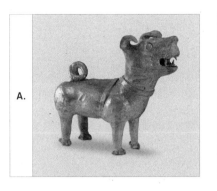

B.

C.

D.

E.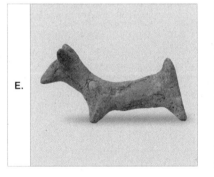

F.

G.

H.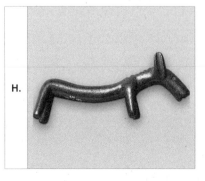

17. Lion Hunts

The stone reliefs shown opposite depict the lion hunts that were popular with Assyrian kings, including Ashurnasirpal II and Ashurbanipal.

Can you use your own hunting skills to spot a single 'LION' hiding in the letter grid below? It may be written in any direction.

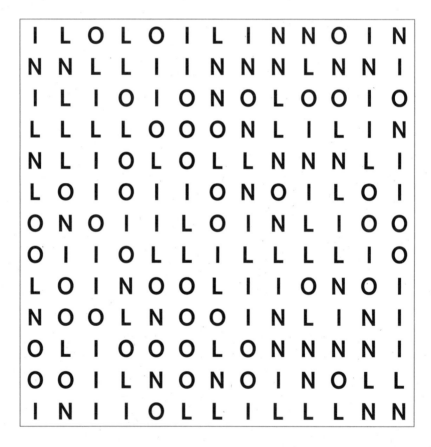

Three gypsum wall panels from ancient Assyria depicting royal lion hunts. Such hunts were symbolic of the ruling monarch's duty to protect and fight for his people.

18. Intoxicating Animals

Despite appearances, each of the objects shown opposite is in fact a 'standing cup', made in the shape of an animal, that can be drunk from.

The names of the six animals that make up the designs of these cups have each been blended below with the name of an alcoholic drink with the same number of letters that could be drunk from that cup, taking alternate letters from each word. For example, ALE and CUP could be blended to give AUE or, if mixed the other way round, CLP.

Can you identify each of the animal and tipple pairs, and then match each animal name to its corresponding image?

		Animal	Drink	Image
1.	WENR			
2.	BTEG			
3.	UAISOLN			
4.	MOAR			
5.	DRANOY			
6.	CECMEUEH			

A.

B.

C.

D.

E.

F.

19. Shape Shifters

According to Amazonian Murui-Muina people, river dolphins are shape-shifters who can disguise themselves as men or women, using other river creatures as their clothing. For example, an electric eel is changed into a belt, fish are made into shoes, and a crab becomes a watch.

Can you similarly change each of the river-dwellers below into a human form by changing one letter per line – and without rearranging the order of the other letters? For example, DOG could become DOT, then COT, then CAT, and so on.

1.

2.

EEL

MAN

CRAB

BOYS

A necklace featuring the teeth of pink river dolphins made by Murui-Muina people.

3.

SHARK

TWINS

4.

BASS

GENT

20. Unusual Figures

The names of the intricately carved animals shown opposite are all listed below. However, they have been obscured by the insertion of extra letters.

Can you delete one letter from each pair to leave just the name of an animal on each line, and then match it to one of the images?

1.   RP LA YT TY LP EP US ND UA CK ED

     Animal: _____   Image: _____

2.   WE CO LH VI DE RN AI SN EO

     Animal: _____   Image: _____

3.   WS QA LU IR UI DS

     Animal: _____   Image: _____

4.   KC UA RT GT AL ER FO IS SO HD

     Animal: _____   Image: _____

5.   KG RI LE AL EY DR   AW HO LA LF SE

     Animal: _____   Image: _____

6.   PA NR GM AO DL IN LI NL OS

     Animal: _____   Image: _____

A.

B.

C.

D.

E.

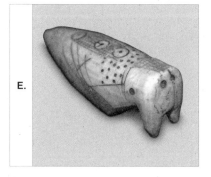

F.

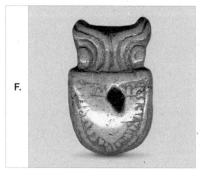

4

Myth and Magic

Throughout history, humans have passed stories from generation to generation, creating legends and myths that help form shared belief systems, cultures and communities. Some stories focus on the realm of the gods, the creation of the world and life after death; others produce monstrous or fantastic creatures to help explain human nature. Many examples can be found in objects in the Museum's collection, including classical gods and goddesses on painted ancient Greek vases, double-headed serpents on Aztec pectorals, and dragons decorating Chinese jars for palaces and temples.

Objects imbued with special meaning and magic become talismanic, carrying with them the power to predict, protect, heal or, indeed, harm. Ancient sources written in a script called cuneiform reveal Mesopotamians trying to speak to ghosts while divination tools from across the world would have been used to tell the future.

1. Missing Mosaic

The highly decorated human skull shown below is said to be the symbol of the Aztec god Tezcatlipoca, also known as 'Smoking Mirror', although some pieces of mosaic are missing.

In the list below, some pieces are also missing from the names of the materials used to decorate the skull. Can you fill in the spaces, writing one letter per gap? The missing letters are given, but also include five extra letters that will remain unused. Once the puzzle is solved, read these extra letters in the order given to discover the role played by 'Smoking Mirror' in Aztec life.

Missing pieces to place:

**C D D E E E E E G I I I I I L
N O R S S T T T U V Y Y**

1.	_ U _ Q _ O _ S _	Mosaic
2.	C _ N _ H _ _ H _ L _	Eyes
3.	P _ R _ T _	Eyes
4.	_ E _ R _ _ K _ N	Lining
5.	L _ G _ I _ E	Mosaic
6.	P _ N _	Adhesive resin
7.	A _ A _ E	Lining

2. Sarcophagus Stack

According to ancient Egyptian beliefs about death and the afterlife, the sarcophagus was the eternal dwelling place of the deceased. Largely made for wealthy citizens, these stone sarcophagi were often built to house smaller wooden coffins, and were intended to remain above ground and on display. The mummy of Tutankhamun, for example, was placed within three nested coffins inside its sarcophagus, and the shrine containing the sarcophagus was itself contained within three nested shrines.

A fragment from the sarcophagus of Ramses VI (above) and the sarcophagus of Pakap (above right).

Try to work out how to nest the fragments of names below inside one another, to reveal the names of five ancient Egyptians whose sarcophagi can be found in the British Museum. For example, the fragment M could be nested inside U _ M, and then again inside M _ _ _ Y to make MUMMY.

A	S_ B	E_ _ _ _ S
A	T_ N	E_ _ _ _ _ B
K	R_ _ O	N_ _ _ _ _ N
O	A_ _ _ E	S_ _ _ _ _ K
Y M	C_ _ _ E	M_ _ _ _ _ _ E
A_ A	E_ _ _ U	N_ _ _ _ _ _ _ O
B_ M	P_ _ _ P	

Write the names in the spaces below:

_ _ _ _ _

_ _ _ _ _

_ _ _ _ _

_ _ _ _ _ _ _

_ _ _ _ _ _ _ _

The wooden coffin of Horaawesheb containing the mummy of a woman.

3. Totem Tales

The K̲'aayáng totem pole, made by Northwest Coast Haida people and shown opposite, has two different stories associated with it. One of those stories has been written out below. The events of the story, however, have been presented in the wrong order.

Work out how to re-order the sentences so that the story is told in chronological order, then read the letter labels that have been added to the start of each sentence. When the sentences have been arranged correctly, these letters will spell out the name of a creature often seen on totem poles, and which is also pictured on the brooch below.

Order
(1–11):

B – Without his beak, Yetl transformed into human form and hid his damaged face.   _____

D – The final figure of Yetl as the wise chief is represented at the top of the totem pole.   _____

D – The villagers baited their new hooks with devil fish and lowered them into the water.   _____

E – Yetl took the bait, and the villagers battled to reel in their catch.   _____

H – The fishhooks – with fish attached – were being taken by the creator figure Yetl.   _____

I – He persuaded the villagers, who accepted him
as a guest, to give back his beak.
_____

N – To try and capture the thief, the villagers began to
make two-pronged fishhooks.
_____

R – They finally pulled the hook from the water, which
had part of Yetl's raven beak attached.
_____

R – With his beak returned, Yetl then reappeared to the
villagers in the form of a wise human chief, and ate
with the villagers.
_____

T – There was once a village whose people lost their
fishhooks each time they fished.
_____

U – Yetl usually took the form of a raven, but was currently
swimming in the water and taking fish for himself.
_____

Carved from cedar wood, this totem pole was made by Haida people
in around 1850. The brooch (opposite), also made by Haida people,
dates from between 1953 and 1968.

4. Totem Tales Too

Totem poles, often made of red cedar wood, may be carved with local legends, historical accounts or kinship lineages. Although no two poles will be exactly alike – with many being crafted by various distinct communities in the Pacific Northwest – several common themes and symbols occur across different designs.

Shown below are six letter-filled 'poles'. Take one letter from each pole, working from left to right, to spell out the names of nine animals often found on the totem poles made by Northwest Peoples. Each letter will be used exactly once, meaning that four words will use just the first four poles, three words will use the first five poles, and two words will use all of the poles. The word 'FISH' has been found already as an example. What are the other eight animals?

B	A	A	E		
B	A	A	F		
E	A	A	G		
F̶	E	G	H̶		
F	E	L	L	E	
R	H	L	L	E	
S	I̶	O	M	E	
W	O	S̶	R	N	N
W	R	V	V	O	R

From left: a model of a totem pole and a totem pole with a doorway carved into its base, both made by Northwest Coast Haida people.

5. Evil Eyes Everywhere

The concept of the 'evil eye' can be found in various different cultures across the world, including ancient Greece, where it was used on pottery made in the 6th century BCE. An evil glare may be given by someone who harbours jealous or resentful feelings towards another, and is said to bring bad luck to the victim. Evil-eye amulets known as 'nazars', such as the ones shown on the opposite page, can be used to ward off the negative energy of an envious or malevolent stare.

Reveal the hidden evil eyes in the grid below by using the number clues to help you locate them. The numbers indicate the exact number of evil eyes in adjacent empty squares, including those that are diagonally adjacent. No more than one eye may be placed in each square, and eyes cannot be placed in squares with numbers. Can you find them all?

2				2		
3		7	4		1	
3				1		1
2			2		2	
	3	2		2		
			2			2
1	2			2	2	

A selection of nazars, or amulets
used to ward off the 'evil eye'.

6. The National God of Rurutu

The figure shown below was found on the French Polynesian island of Rurutu, and is thought to depict the Rurutu creator god. Carbon dating has revealed that it was sculpted around 400 years ago.

Find out more about this statue by completing each of the partially written words opposite with one of the double-letter pairs that have been given. The remaining unused pair can be used to complete the final line, thus revealing the name of the god.

Letter pairs to place:

AA   EE   LL   LL   LL   OO   PP   RR   SS   SS

- The figure is thought to be made of S A N D A L W _ _ D

- The figure's F _ _ T and lower legs are missing

- The statue is H O _ _ O W at the back and features a removable lid

- The cavity may have been used to store the S K U _ _ or bones of a significant ancestor

- When used, the figure may then have been W R A _ _ E D with feathered cord

- The statue may have been polished with coconut oil and cowrie S H E _ _ S

- The statue was taken by M I _ _ I O N A R I E S and brought to London

- The statue has travelled to various cities on exhibition, including Paris and C A N B E _ _ A

- The statue has been copied many times: the artist P I C A _ _ O owned a version

The god depicted by the statue is _ ' _ , supreme deity of the island of Rurutu.

7. Incantation Bowl

Incantation bowls, like the one shown opposite, have been found across the Middle East and were used for protective magic. Spells were written inside the bowls, which were then buried face-down in order to trap evil or malevolent spirits.

Mentally rotate each of the nested bowls below so that six words that solve the clues opposite line up simultaneously, when read outwards from the centre. Each six-letter word can then be written next to its description.

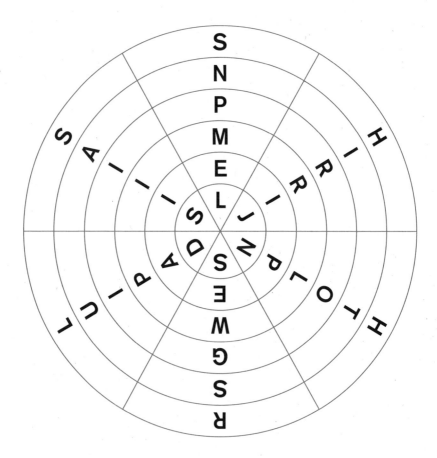

L _ _ _ _ _   Biblical figure cited as the first wife of Adam, banished from Eden and considered an evil spirit

J _ _ _ _ _   Dialect of Babylonian Aramaic found on most incantation bowls

N _ _ _ _ _   Sumerian city where multiple bowls were found buried

S _ _ _ _ _   Shape in which most incantations were written

D _ _ _ _ _   Malevolent spirits from whom incantation bowls offered protection

S _ _ _ _ _   Name of the beneficiary inscribed on the bowl shown here

8. Omnipresent Goddesses

In many of the world's mythologies, deities are divided between masculine and feminine genders, with the two camps typically having both benevolent and fearsome representatives. But whether male or female, good or evil, the vast range of historical artefacts dedicated to deities are testament to the long-standing and omnipresent belief in these awe-inspiring, powerful beings.

All of the ancient goddesses clued below also exhibit 'omnipresence' in their names — although in this case it means simply that they begin and end with the same letter. Complete each of their names by identifying this repeated missing letter, and then match each deity's name to one of the artefacts shown opposite, labelled A to I.

The nine missing letters, each used twice per name, are:

A A D I S S T T U

Artefact

1.	__ A T I __	Egyptian goddess of the flood	_____
2.	__ N A H I T __	Iranian water goddess	_____
3.	__ P E __	Roman goddess of hope	_____
4.	__ T H E N __	Greek goddess of wisdom	_____
5.	__ A N I __	Punic goddess of Carthage	_____
6.	__ T T __	Mesopotamian goddess associated with weaving and spiders	_____
7.	__ Z A N A M __	Japanese goddess of creation	_____
8.	__ R Y A __	One of several tree nymphs in Greek mythology	_____
9.	__ A W E R E __	Egyptian goddess of childbirth	_____

A.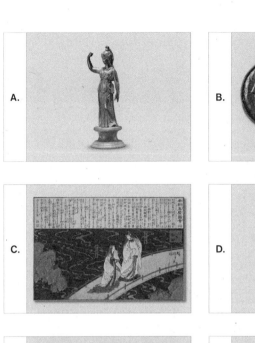

B.

C.

D.

E.

F.

G.

H.

I.

9. Dr Dee's Crystal Ball

John Dee was an English alchemist and would-be sorcerer, born in 1527. During the course of his career he amassed several 'magical' objects, including the crystal ball and magic mirror shown here.

Using only the letters found in Dr Dee's crystal ball, opposite, solve the clues below to divine more information on the artefacts. Each floating letter should be used exactly once.

_ _ _ _ _   Heavenly creature who supposedly gave
                             Dee his crystal ball

_ _ _ _ _ _   Mesoamerican origin of Dee's magic
                             mirror

_ _ _ _ _ _ _ _ _   English queen who demanded to see
                             Dee's crystal ball in use

_ _ _ _ _ _   Polish city where Dee's apprentice
                             experienced a vision

_ _ _ _ _ _ _ _   Volcanic glass material used for Dee's
                             magic mirror

Some of the objects connected with John Dee, including his magic mirror and crystal ball (first and second from left).

10. Day of the Dead 1

Listed below are items that might be placed on an *ofrenda* during celebrations for the Day of the Dead, or Día de los Muertos, in Mexico. *Ofrendas* are altars set up in family homes, featuring objects intended to welcome and celebrate the spirits of deceased ancestors.

Place each of the items into the grid opposite, writing one letter per box, so each word reads either left to right or down the page. When complete, the shaded squares will spell out, from top to bottom, the name of the female figure shown in the bottom right-hand corner of this page, who features prominently in Day of the Dead imagery.

4 letters
BELL
COMB
SALT
SOAP

5 letters
BREAD
COPAL
CROSS
FRUIT
SEEDS
WATER

6 letters
CANDLE

7 letters
TEQUILA

9 letters
CHOCOLATE
STATUETTE

10 letters
PHOTOGRAPH
SUGAR SKULL

11 letters
TISSUE PAPER

Name of figure above:

_____

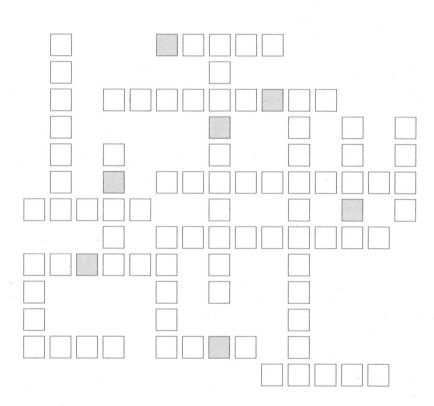

A selection of objects that might appear on an *ofrenda*, a miniature version of which is shown opposite (bottom left).

11. Day of the Dead 2

An important part of Day of the Dead celebrations are *papel picado*: pieces of paper decorated with perforated designs through which the souls of the dead may travel.

In the descriptions below, some words have also been perforated and the 'punched out' groups of letters collected. Can you place each punched-out letter group back into one of the resulting perforations, thus restoring the words and solving their associated clues?

Punched-out letter groups:

AL	AR	EM	IB	IX	NOV	RU
SK	TO	US	VE	XIC	ZC	ZO

Word	Clue
ME _ _ _ O	Country associated with the Day of the Dead
_ _ _ _ _ _ BER	The month in which Día de los Muertos falls
C _ _ A _ _ RA	Spanish name for a traditional sugar skull
ME _ _ _ AL	Alcoholic spirit sometimes included as part of an *ofrenda*
C _ _ CIF _ _	Catholic symbol sometimes placed on an *ofrenda*
H _ _ ISC _ _	Exotic flower from which traditional tea is made
_ _ ELE _ _ N	Shape of traditional calacas figurines
_ _ I _ _ NA	US state that holds a Day of the Dead procession

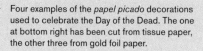

Four examples of the *papel picado* decorations used to celebrate the Day of the Dead. The one at bottom right has been cut from tissue paper, the other three from gold foil paper.

12. Hindu Deities

Hinduism – one of the world's oldest continuously practised religions – can be described as a system of thought and practice that first developed in the Indian subcontinent several millennia ago. There are multiple branches and sects, and a number of Hindu deities are common to many of these distinct denominations. Some of them are listed below.

Fit the names of these gods and goddesses into the grid opposite so that an ancient spiritual word is revealed. Write one letter per box so that every deity's name can be read horizontally across one of the rows of boxes. Some boxes span multiple words, indicating shared letters. Once complete, the letters in the shaded squares will reveal, when read from top to bottom, the Sanskrit name given to the bodily manifestation of a divine being.

BRAHMA

DURGA

GANESHA

HANUMAN

HARIHARA

KALI

KARTIKEYA

KRISHNA

LAKSHMI

PARVATI

SARASVATI

SHIVA

VISHNU

Sanskrit word:

_____

From top: a small statue of Krishna playing
the flute, and two depictions of Ganesha.

13. Masked Meaning

Masks have been worn in many different cultures for thousands of years, for many different purposes. Some of the masks in the British Museum's collection are shown opposite, with each mask depicting a specific figure with its own spiritual significance.

Below, the subject of each of these masks – either an animal or an ancestor – has been 'masked' by overlaying the name of the place from which that mask originates. Are you able to identify both the place and the subject of each mask, and then match this information to one of the masks labelled A to E?

DRAGON

Place: _____ Subject: _____ Mask: _____

REDFOX

Place: _____ Subject: _____ Mask: _____

CANADA

Place: _____ Subject: _____ Mask: _____

NEWCALEDONIA

Place: _____ Subject: _____ Mask: _____

OAKANCESTOR

Place: _____ Subject: _____ Mask: _____

A.

B.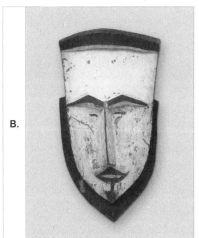

C.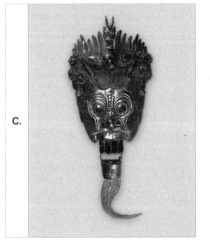

D.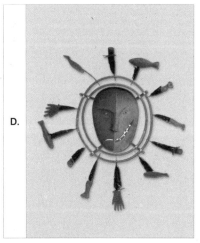

E.

14. The Rivers of Eden

On the amulet opposite, the names of the four rivers of Eden – as described in the book of Genesis – have been written several times over. Intriguingly, they can be read forwards, backwards and in several anagrammed forms, on both sides of the amulet.

Try to find the English names of the four rivers of Eden in the grid below. The names may be written in any direction, including diagonally, and read either forwards or backwards, but each name can only be found once, at least in a non-anagrammed form. The names to find are as follows:

CHIDEKEL   GIHON   PERAT   PISHON

H	G	A	E	A	A	T	R	A	H	N	C	K	D	T
G	T	I	P	R	I	D	I	H	D	T	E	T	O	E
P	E	K	C	H	T	H	T	I	K	A	L	K	O	N
R	T	D	L	S	I	A	E	G	G	O	S	G	T	D
A	G	T	T	R	L	H	A	L	S	G	A	T	O	T
O	E	H	P	K	G	P	S	E	D	G	O	L	A	H
H	D	H	I	S	G	I	S	L	I	S	L	L	O	T
A	H	E	N	C	D	T	C	K	E	T	E	L	R	T
K	O	O	H	O	O	C	T	T	A	D	K	O	L	D
T	D	K	O	S	H	P	D	R	R	P	E	D	A	C
P	G	C	R	C	T	S	E	I	N	P	D	L	A	A
H	C	I	A	K	H	P	I	O	L	S	I	C	G	I
S	G	N	H	K	A	A	E	P	H	N	H	E	H	I
R	D	H	T	O	G	N	O	T	C	P	C	H	N	P
K	I	R	E	O	N	L	S	P	D	D	O	R	O	O

Inscribed in Hebrew, this amulet (both sides of which are shown) is thought to date from the
18th century. The rivers of Eden are said to bear the stream of life out of the Garden of Eden.

15. Fishy Tales

The British Museum is home to around 50,000 drawings and more than 2 million prints from around the world. Four such items from its collection are shown on pages 128–129, each depicting a scene or character from a tale with a somewhat fishy nature.

Each of these tales is summarized in the four numbered paragraphs below. Words in capital letters, however, have been anagrammed. Can you unscramble them to reveal the true details of each story? Once you have solved the anagrams, match each tale to the image that was made to illustrate it.

1. After angering the SNEAK goddess Manasa, a man was killed by

    PRESENTS. His wife, Behula, refused to MERECAT his body. Instead,

    she tried to bring him back to life by carrying him through a great

    IRVRE. The husband's KEEN was then eaten by one of the fish. After

    appeasing the gods, it was agreed that Behula's husband could be

    STEERCRUDER. This was done, but only after the KEEN was taken

    from the stomach of the fish who WASLEDOWL it.

    Image: _____

2. A man named Tametomo and his family were caught in a great

    TROSM at sea, which is said to have been caused by a vengeful

    GODRAN. To appease the gods, his wife decided to FAIRIESCC

    herself to the sea. Tametomo and his son found refuge on the back

    of a huge ASHKR. They were saved by tengu – beings that are part

    DIBR and part MAHNU.

    Image: _____

3. After a brief adventure on the NOMO, a man named Lucian and his group return to HEART. While swimming in a calm sea, they are swallowed by a AWLHE. Inside the beast, they find TERSE, birds and BSHRE. The group kill the creature that swallowed them by starting a FINEORB in its stomach. They manage to escape by PIPPORNG its mouth open.

    Image: _____

4. As a young boy, the RIARROW Benkei was known as Oniwaka. Whilst studying in a PELMET, Oniwaka discovered that a giant PARC had killed his mother. His mother had fallen off the edge of the large ALTARFLEW, and been killed in the LOOP at the bottom. Onikawa used his extraordinary GHENTSTR to kill the beast, and GENEVA his mother's death.

    Image: _____

DID YOU KNOW ...?

The British Museum's collection of prints and drawings includes works by some of the world's greatest graphic artists, from Albrect Dürer, Hokusai and Mary Delany to Michelangelo, Käthe Kollwitz and Pablo Picasso.

Continued overleaf →

A.

Continued
from
previous
page

B.

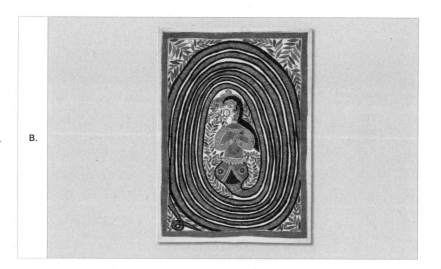

C.

D.

16. Gods of Chaos

Not all gods are made equal, and several mythologies around the world feature gods of chaos who are responsible for destruction, harm and disorder. The word 'chaos' is in fact taken from the name of Chaos, the first created being in Greek mythology, from whom all the other primeval deities were themselves created.

Make sense of the chaotic arrangement of floating letters below by joining each god of chaos on the left with the mythology it pertains to on the right. To do so, use straight lines to join the corresponding dots, with each dot used exactly once, and each line passing through a single letter. Then, read the crossed-through letters from top to bottom to reveal the name of an animal considered to be a symbol of chaos in the ancient world. What is it?

Discordia •   T   • Aztec

           E K

Eris •   L   • Egyptian

       H   A

Juracan •   N   • Greek

      S   G

Nammu •   T   • Irish

           E

Set • O   • Mesopotamian

The Formorians •   L O   • Roman

Tiamat •   U   • Sumerian

       E   T P

Tlaltecuhtli •   M   • Taino

From top: a piece of pottery featuring Eris, a cylinder
seal depicting Tiamat, and a print also showing Eris.

17. Snake Link

Snakes can be found at the heart of many different myths and belief systems around the world, from creation stories to the biblical tale of the fall of man. Gods and goddesses from a wide variety of cultures are also often depicted as snakes.

Can you use your logic skills to uncover the names of several more snake deities from across the world that have been split up in the grid below? To do so, join the two halves of each snake deity's name by drawing a path between a pair of circles, so that all the circles are joined into pairs. Only one path can enter each square, so paths cannot cross; they can also only travel horizontally or vertically between squares. To work out which circles should be joined into pairs, use the guide opposite, which provides the first and last letters of each god's name, along with the number of letters in its name, alongside their mythology. Once you have joined the circles, you can then fill in the missing letters in each of their names.

A _ _ P   Egyptian god of death, embodied as a snake

C _ _ _ A   Serpent goddess in Irish mythology

D _ _ _ _ I   Supreme god of Fijian mythology and creator of
                 Fijian islands

F _ _ I   Creation god in Chinese mythology, depicted with
                 a snake's tail

G _ B   Egyptian god of the earth, considered to be the father
                 of snakes

H _ _ _ _ A   Sea serpent in Greek mythology

N _ _ A   A name for part-human, part-serpent deities in Hinduism

W _ _ _ _ L   Name for the Aboriginal Rainbow Serpent used by
                 the Noongar in Australia

Rubbing of a Han dynasty stone relief decorated with a snake-bodied deity (left)
and a nagakal (right), stone tablets found in southern India devoted to snake deities.

18. Rings of Magic

Wearable amulets and talismans, thought to offer the wearer protection from harm, are found in cultures the world over in the form of jewellery. Rings engraved with healing inscriptions, or set with stones believed to offer medicinal protection, provide insight into the spiritual and scientific practices of civilizations from ancient Egypt to the modern day.

Use the ring-shaped grid opposite to help fill in the missing words in the following descriptions of the magical rings depicted on page 136. To do so, trace a single path that visits every letter in the grid exactly once, spelling out the missing words as you go. Move only horizontally or vertically between touching letters, beginning at the shaded square and finishing in one of the two squares next to it. The words are clued in the same order in which they can be found in the grid.

Ring:

1. This ring with a magical Old English runic inscription was found in   ____

   __ __ __ __ __ __ __

2. This ring with astrological symbols is inscribed with the names of   ____
   the angels Sadayel, Tiriel and __ __ __ __ __ __ __

3. The underside of this Egyptian swivelling ring features a hidden   ____
   image of a __ __ __ __ __ __ __

4. This brass warrior talisman ring is from the Indonesian island of   ____

   __ __ __ __ __ __

5. This bronze amulet ring is inscribed with the name of the angel   ____

   __ __ __ __ __

6. This gold ring has a Latin inscription associated with   ____

   __ __ __ __ __ __

7. This amulet ring, which may have been used to protect against kidney disease, features a mythical _ _ _ _ _ _ _ _ _ _ .

8. This opal ring inscribed with charms also features images of two _ _ _ _ _ _ _ _ _

Once you have found all the missing words, try to match each description to one of the rings shown overleaf, labelled A to H.

C	A	I	S	P	H	A	E
S	R	L	L	A	R	O	L
R	E	T	E	R	P	C	S
O	N	S			I	O	N
M	O	T			T	A	S
E	N	S	R	O	R	M	U
O	A	D	C	X	A	A	N
T	M	S	I	E	L	E	A

Continued overleaf

A.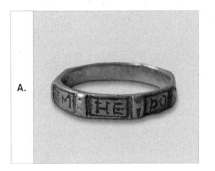

B.

C.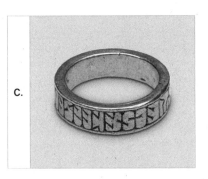

D.

E.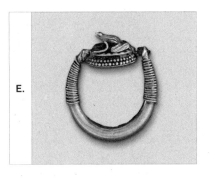

F.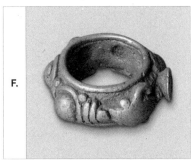

G.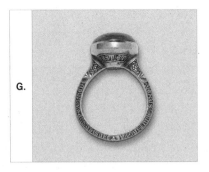

H.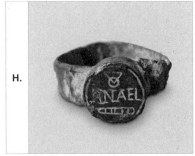

Continued from previous page

19. Magic Squares of Mars

A 'magic square' is a grid of non-repeating numbers in which every row, column and long diagonal adds up to the same number. They have been known about since at least 190 BCE, and in Western occult tradition magic squares were linked to planets and other celestial bodies; the sun, for example, was linked to a 6×6 square, and Saturn to a 3×3 square. Amulets bearing the magic square of a particular astronomical body were thought to give specific protections to the wearer.

Fill in the blank squares below to complete the magic square of Mars, which appears on the back of the amulet shown in the bottom right-hand corner of this page. The sum of each row, column and both long diagonals must equal 65, with each number from 1 to 25 used just once.

	24		20	
4		25		16
	5	13	21	
10		1		22
	6	19	2	

Brass amulet made in Europe between the 16th and 18th centuries. The planetary symbol and seal of Mars are shown above and below the figure of a man.

20. The Nasca Lines

The artefacts shown in the lower half of the page opposite were created more than 2,000 years ago by Nasca people in what is now modern-day Peru. Nasca people, however, are best known for their massive geoglyphs etched into the surrounding land, which are only recognizable as images when viewed from above. Many of the geometric shapes create images of animals and figures that are thought to have spiritual significance, although the original purpose of the shapes is unknown.

Make your own geoglyph in the square below by connecting all of the dots to form a single loop. The loop cannot cross or touch itself at any point, and only horizontal and vertical lines between dots are allowed. Some parts of the loop have already been given.

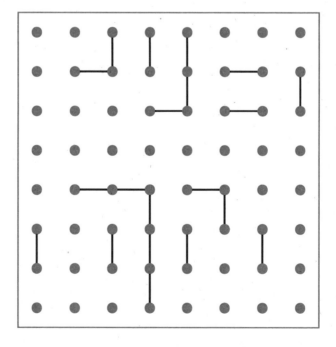

A geoglyph in the shape of a spider (top), two pottery
vessels (centre) and a large textile fragment (bottom right),
all attributed to Nasca people.

5

The Written Word

Different writing systems were created independently all over the world. The oldest examples of writing date from around 5,000 years ago and are found on clay tablets from ancient Mesopotamia, written in cuneiform. Other scripts were invented in India, Egypt, China and Central America at around the same time. Each script takes its own form and looks completely different, but they are all ways of visually recording language.

From its earliest days, writing has been used for the most mundane of tasks, such as list-making and record-keeping, as well as the telling of great works of literature and poetry. Both alphabetic and pictorial forms were created – one of the most famous scripts combining both systems being ancient Egyptian hieroglyphs, which were deciphered using one of the Museum's most famous objects, the Rosetta Stone. The oldest form of writing still in use today is Chinese.

1. An Increasing Problem

The tablet shown below, made of the mineral gypsum, was discovered in what is now the country of Iraq. Artefacts of this type are nicknamed 'bug-eyed monster' tablets thanks to their appearance, although the imprinted lines and dots on the plaster encode an ancient numbering system. Specifically, each dot represents a certain number of lines, in a similar way to the stacking of units, tens and hundreds in modern numerals.

Complete the number pyramid below to reveal the age of the ancient number tablet. Write a number in every empty brick, so that each brick contains a value equal to the sum of the two bricks immediately beneath it, where present. The number in the shaded square at the top of the pyramid will reveal the approximate year BCE in which the tablet was produced.

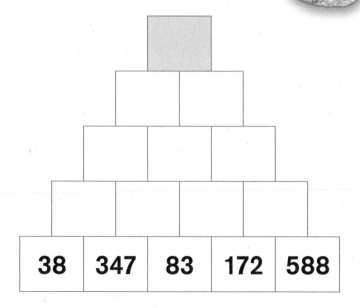

| 38 | 347 | 83 | 172 | 588 |

2. Un-written in Stone

This Roman inscription is a votive dedication to several members of the same family, some of whom were rulers within the Roman Empire. The story does not end happily, however: one of those named may have ordered the deaths of two others on the votive. The names of the deceased were then removed from the stone-written dedication, in a process known as *damnatio memoriae*.

Complete the wordsearch opposite in order to find out which unlucky family members were 'damned from memory'. In the translation of the inscription below, all of the names and roles written in capital letters can be found in the grid, except for the names of the two people who were erased. Words may be written in any direction, and names consisting of two words appear next to each other without a space between them. Which two people can no longer be found?

'To FORTUNA, PROTECTRESS of the EMPERORS, ANTONIUS,

FREEDMAN and imperial SECRETARY for petitions, dedicates this as

a gift, from a vow made, for the wellbeing and safe return of our emperors

SEVERUS PIUS and ANTONINUS PIUS and PRINCE GETA and the

EMPRESS JULIA, MOTHER of the emperors and EMPRESS PLAUTILLA.'

```
H V O Q U V N F G S L D R S
G E F T J T J R P F P E E Z
S L C N J M Q A E W H V A B
W U J T R P T Q B T E H S U
I V I J M J V C O R L K J P
L A L P Q E X M U X D N S D
S H I X S D Q S U N W U W P
S R X L Z U P U S T I R R J
E U O F U I N P F N P O U S
C F Z R U J X I O M T Z P A
R R Y S E J S T N E M M N Y
E E B W Z P N S C O Y U C P
T E V B F A M T E E T E J P
A D N V J G R E C R G N L J
R M R S P E X X O N P A A X
Y A M Y S O U F X D L M Y M
E N S S J M N D I I Z M E Y
```

Erased people:

_____

_____

3. The Handscroll of Admonitions

Believed to have been made in China between the 5th and 7th centuries CE, the scroll pictured below is a beautifully illustrated version of the poem 'Admonitions of the Instructress to the Court Ladies'. This section of the scroll depicts a hypothetical emperor surrounded by his family in a scene of domestic harmony.

The text opposite is an approximate translation of the poetic Chinese words that accompany the image, although with an important difference: those words written in capital letters have been replaced with anagrams. Try to unjumble each of these words to reveal an English translation of the text that accompanies this scene.

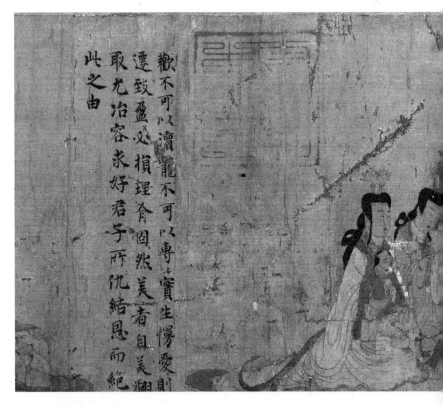

Detail of a handscroll painting in nine scenes (originally twelve) illustrating 'Admonitions of the Instructress to the Court Ladies', a text composed by Zhang Hua in the 3rd century CE.

'To utter a word, how light a NIGHT that seems! Yet from a word,

both NOHOUR and AMESH proceed. Do not think that that you are

HINDED; For the INVIED mirror CLEFREST even that which cannot be

seen. Do not think that you have been LIONESSES; God's ERA needs

no NODUS. Do not SOBAT of your glory; For heaven's law HASTE

what is full. Do not put your STRUT in honours and high birth; For he that

is HEIGHTS falls. Make the "Little TSARS" your NETTRAP. Do not let

your FIANCES AMOR afar. Let your EARTHS be as the CUTLOSS

And your CARE shall multiply.'

4. Alphabetical Zeal

Listed below are the names of five alphabets, one per line, but with their letters arranged in alphabetical order so as to disguise them.

Are you able to unscramble the names, and then match each alphabet to an artefact on the opposite page that features the script in question?

	Alphabet:	Artefact:
1. ACENRSTU		
2. AILNT		
3. BEEHRW		
4. CINRU		
5. EEGKR		

DID YOU KNOW ...?

One of the oldest examples of the use of an alphabet dates from around 1800 BCE. A small statue of a sphinx found in Egypt bears an inscription in the Proto-Sinaitic script, which, via the Phoenician alphabet, gave rise to many modern alphabets.

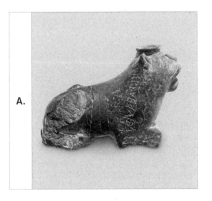

A.

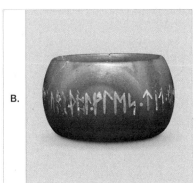

B.

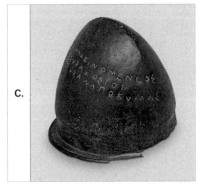

C.

D.

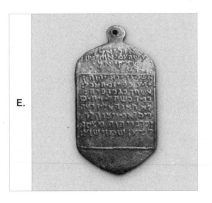

E.

5. The Franks Casket

The densely decorated Franks casket, the front and back of which is shown opposite, is thought to have been created in 8th-century England. Several stories are depicted on its outer panels, including biblical tales, a Roman myth and a native Germanic legend known as 'Weland the Smith'. There are also inscriptions in both runic and Latin alphabets, switching between Old English and Latin – and even Latin text in runic script. Some of the inscriptions have also been deliberately written upside down or back to front.

The front panel includes an Old English riddle, encircling the outer edges of the pictorial content. The solution to the riddle – also written on the front of the casket – reveals what material the casket is made from. To find out yourself, can you complete your own looped pattern in the square below? Join all of the dots to form a single loop that visits each dot exactly once, while using only horizontal or vertical lines. When complete, the looped route will pass over some of the letters; read these letters clockwise around the loop, starting from the top-left corner, to reveal the answer:

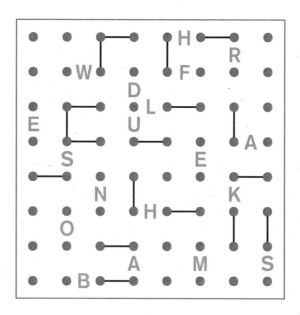

The Franks Casket is also known as the Auzon Casket. Scars on the exterior of the casket, such as the one on its front, indicate lost metal fittings, including a lock and handle.

6. Reading the Runes

The Franks Casket is well known for the Old English riddle written in runes on its front panel, seen in the image below.

Use the number clues opposite to reveal the runes that spell the first word of that riddle, by shading certain squares. These clues provide, when read from left to right or top to bottom, the length of every run of consecutive shaded squares in each row and column. There must be a gap of at least one empty square between each run of shaded squares in the same row or column.

Just as the casket is carved in low relief, the area you shade will become the background and the runes will appear in the foreground. Beneath the runes, an image representing the runic word's meaning will also be revealed.

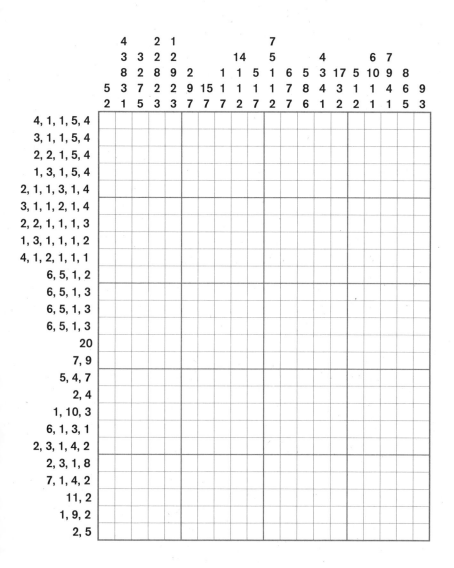

Column clues (top):

```
  4     2 1                7
  3  3  2 2         14      5        4          6  7
  8  2  8 9  2      1  1  5 1  6  5  3 17  5 10  9  8
5 3  7  2 2  9 15 1 1  1  1 1  7  8  4  3  1  1  4  6  9
2 1  5  3 3  7  7 7 7  2  7 2  7  6  1  2  2  1  1  5  3
```

Row clues (left):

- 4, 1, 1, 5, 4
- 3, 1, 1, 5, 4
- 2, 2, 1, 5, 4
- 1, 3, 1, 5, 4
- 2, 1, 1, 3, 1, 4
- 3, 1, 1, 2, 1, 4
- 2, 2, 1, 1, 1, 3
- 1, 3, 1, 1, 1, 2
- 4, 1, 2, 1, 1, 1
- 6, 5, 1, 2
- 6, 5, 1, 3
- 6, 5, 1, 3
- 6, 5, 1, 3
- 20
- 7, 9
- 5, 4, 7
- 2, 4
- 1, 10, 3
- 6, 1, 3, 1
- 2, 3, 1, 4, 2
- 2, 3, 1, 8
- 7, 1, 4, 2
- 11, 2
- 1, 9, 2
- 2, 5

7. The Epic Library

The clay tablet shown opposite is taken from a famous Assyrian library in the city of Nineveh that at one time held around 30,000 similar texts. The majority of the tablets are inscribed with cuneiform script in the Akkadian language; this particular tablet is a record of three spells that could be recited for protection against sorcery and demons. Somewhat ironically, the library itself was preserved by something intending to destroy it: a fire, which inadvertently baked the clay tablets solid.

The library is named after the last great Assyrian king, but can you use the grid below to reveal his name? Place a letter from the set A, B, E, H, I, L, N, P, R, S, T and U into each empty square, so that no letter repeats in any row, column or bold-lined 4×3 box. Once all the boxes have been filled, the name of the library's founder will be spelled out in the shaded diagonal, reading from top to bottom.

		N		B	L	I	S		H		
		E	T					L	A		
B	P									U	I
	I			E			A			P	
S			B		N	P		T			U
R				L			U				H
N				U			P				R
U			E		T	B		S			P
	T			H			R			N	
T	R									E	S
		U	I					R	B		
		S		A	R	H	T		N		

This tablet, which dates from the 7th century BCE, was found by Sir Austen Henry Layard, an archaeologist and politician credited with excavating Nineveh in the late 1840s/early 1850s.

8. The Epic Poem

The clay tablet opposite, created in the 7th century BCE, depicts part of an epic poem. It is perhaps the most famous artefact written in cuneiform, since the tale it tells is remarkably similar to the story of the Great Flood in the book of Genesis.

An abridged translation of the portion of the poem featured on the tablet is given below, although the sentences have been listed in the wrong order. Work out how to rearrange them so that the passage is told in chronological order. Once the sentences are in the correct order, the letter given at the start of each line will spell out the name of the ancient hero who gives his name to the entire epic poem.

Order (1–9)

A – The boat was to have very specific dimensions, and to be made with wood, oil and bitumen.   _____

E – The gods then sent their secret storm, which raged for six days and six nights, destroying humanity and shattering the earth 'like a pot'.   _____

G – He told Utnapishtim to dismantle his house and build a boat in which he could escape the flood, along with several other living creatures.   _____

G – The immortal Utnapishtim tells the hero of how he gained his eternal life.   _____

H – After some initial anger that a living being had survived the extinction event, the gods eventually bestowed immortality on Utnapishtim and his wife, who were transported to the mouth of the river Euphrates to live there for ever.   _____

I – Five of the great gods had hatched a secret plan to bring about the destruction of humankind.   _____

L – One of those gods, Ea, told Utnapishtim about the plan, which would take the form of a giant flood.

M – Utnapishtim loaded the boat with his wife and relatives, food and provisions, and as many living animals as he could.

S – After the storm, Utnapishtim sailed until he could find land, setting his livestock free and gaining the attention of the gods.

Hero: _____

Fragment of the Neo-Assyrian clay tablet known as 'the Flood Tablet'.

9. Characterful Creation

On several of the 'pages' of this Chinese book, engraved on to leaves of jade, are the re-imaginings of ancient Chinese characters. Each novel character – designed with lines of fixed width, and often in geometric arrangements – is paired with the traditional character it is imitating.

Can you similarly match up each pair of identical digits opposite, where one digit in each pair is shown in a standard appearance and the other in a more fanciful style? To do so, draw paths to join each pair in such a way that only one path enters each square, which means that paths cannot cross. Paths can only travel horizontally or vertically between squares.

This jade book, composed of seven leaves and two covers (not shown), was produced in 1748 during the reign of the Qianlong Emperor.

1	2		3					
			4					
5	1							
			5			6		
		7						
	8			9				
			3					
	8			9			4	
	7	2				6		

10. Cyrus's Cylinder

The cylindrical tablet shown opposite is inscribed with Babylonian text written in cuneiform script. Known as the Cyrus Cylinder, it recounts the arrival in Babylon of the benevolent king Cyrus, detailing his conquest of the city and his undoing of years of ungodly and unfair rule in the region. The text shows that the tablet was written to be buried in the city wall of Babylon, where it was deposited after the capture of the city by Cyrus in 539 BCE.

Mentally rotate each of the nested discs below so that six words that solve the clues opposite line up simultaneously, when read outwards from the centre. Each six-letter word can then be written next to its description.

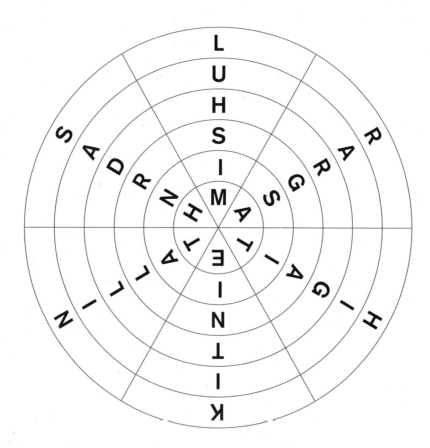

M _ _ _ _ _   God loved by Cyrus, who helped him with his conquest

A _ _ _ _ _   Ancient Persian city in which Cyrus was born and which he later reigned over

T _ _ _ _ _   One of two ancient rivers of Mesopotamia, the other being the Euphrates

E _ _ _ _ _   Name of the Babylonian temple dedicated to the aforementioned god

T _ _ _ _ _   Traditional Sumerian name for Babylon

H _ _ _ _ _   Modern city in Iraq, on the site of ancient Babylon

Made after 539 BCE, this object's cylindrical form is typical of royal inscriptions of the Late Babylonian period.

11. Roman Occupations

The people whose names are listed below were all occupants of a garrison on the northern frontier of the Roman empire in Britain, around 100 CE. Details of their lives, both professional and personal, can be found in the Vindolanda Tablets – a set of wooden tablets uncovered in remarkable condition in Northumberland that provide an unrivalled account of day-to-day life in Roman Britain.

Place each name into a row of the grid opposite, writing one letter per empty box, to reveal that person's occupation as described in the tablets. Once the grid has been completed, the letters in the shaded column will spell out the full name of a woman who invited Sulpicia Lepidina to her birthday party – the earliest known writing by a woman in Latin (below).

AELIUS	MARCUS
ALIO	PRIVATUS
ARECTUS	RHENUS
FLAVIUS	VELDEDIUS
GAVO	VIRILIS
GENTILIS	VITALIS
LUCIUS	

The wooden writing tablet from Vindolanda that contains a party invitation to Sulpicia Lepidina.

	A					
				O		
	V					
			C			
E						
				I		
					U	

Doctor

Veterinary surgeon

Pharmacist

Shieldmaker

Groom

Freedman

Prefect

			U			
				N		
		A				
				T		
			I			
					S	

Prefect

Slave

Clothing supplier

Brewer

Veterinary surgeon

Slave

Writer's name: _____

More fragments of the wooden writing tablets found in the former Roman fort of Vindolanda.

12. Etruscan Enigma

The Etruscan language, spoken by inhabitants of what is now Tuscany between 700 BCE and 20 CE, had its own writing system. Similar to a proto-Greek alphabet, the Etruscan lettering used a phonological system to capture speech sounds. Relatively few examples of Etruscan inscription survive, making the language difficult to study and understand.

E	T	R	U
N	A	C	S
:	I	N	S
P	I	R	C
T	I	O	N
E	W	:	S
R	E	:	O
N	E	T	F
:	I	N	:
S	U	O	B
T	R	O	P
O	D	E	H
N	:	S	T
:	E	L	Y

Try to decipher a key fact about Etruscan writings by using this letter grid. The text is written in English, but it's up to you to work out how the inscription – written in an Etruscan style – should otherwise be read. It may help to know that a colon was often used to separate Etruscan words.

An item of pottery (top) and a bronze plaque featuring rare examples of Etruscan writing.

13. The Rosetta Stone

The Rosetta Stone (shown on page 165) – perhaps the British Museum's most iconic artefact – is best known for having provided the key to deciphering Egyptian hieroglyphs, thereby unlocking the hitherto unknown ways of life of an ancient civilization. The writing on the stone is split into three sections, although there are only two languages inscribed: Greek and Egyptian. The first two parts, at the top of the stone, show two different writing systems used for ancient Egyptian.

Can you crack the three codes overleaf to reveal information about the three writing systems inscribed on the Rosetta Stone, and which are used on the stone in the same order in which the codes are given? Each numbered section (1 to 3) has had a different 'Caesar shift' encryption applied to it, meaning that all of the letters in that section have been shifted by a consistent amount through the alphabet. The word 'ALPHABET' shifted forward one place, for example, would become BMQIBCFU, since A becomes B, L becomes M, and so on, wrapping around from Z to A. It is up to you to identify what the actual shifts are for each of the three sections.

DID YOU KNOW ...?

The Rosetta Stone has been on display at the British Museum since 1802, with only one exception. During the First World War, to protect it from air raids on London, it was moved to a station on the Post Office Underground Railway at Holborn.

Continued overleaf

**LMIVSKPCTLMG
WGVMTX YWIH FC
TVMIWXW**

— 1

**FGOQVKE UETKRV HQT
GXGTAFCA YTKVKPIU**

— 2

**HSWOHILAPJ NYLLR
MVY HKTPUPZAYHAPVU**

— 3

Decoded text: Shift:

1. _____   _____

2. _____   _____

3. _____   _____

Continued from previous page

Produced in 196 BCE, the Rosetta Stone was found in 1799 by soldiers in Napoleon's army while they were digging the foundations of an addition to a fort near the town of el-Rashid in Egypt.

14. The Crossword Block

Featuring an inscription in Egyptian hieroglyphs dedicated to the goddess Mut, the remarkable stone block shown opposite is known as the 'Crossword' Stela. It was designed to be read in three different directions; however, although it can be read from right to left and vertically, lost details around the edge of the stone make it impossible to read the script in a third way.

Try to complete these two-way modern-day crosswords, where the solution to each clue can be read both across (i.e. left to right) and down the corresponding row and column.

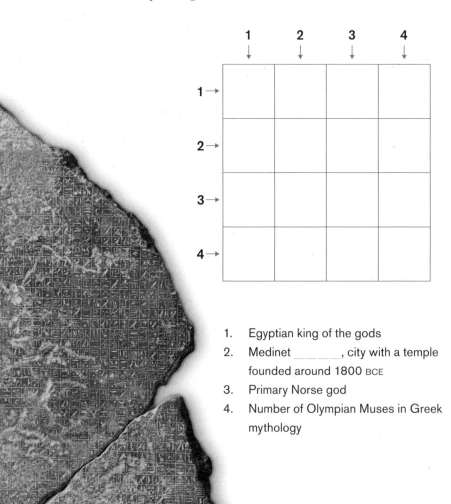

1. Egyptian king of the gods
2. Medinet _____, city with a temple founded around 1800 BCE
3. Primary Norse god
4. Number of Olympian Muses in Greek mythology

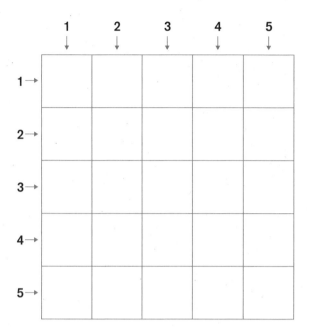

1. Country whose modern capital is Cairo
2. Birds sacred to the ancient civilization of clue 1
3. Country bordering the Red Sea
4. A pretentious, false intellectual
5. Cares for, perhaps, a flock of clue 2

The 'Crossword' Stela (left; detail shown opposite) dates from the 20th Dynasty of Egypt (1189 to 1077 BCE).

15. A List of Kings

The stone carvings pictured opposite – taken from the temple of Ramesses II in Abydos – list the names of several kings of ancient Egypt, up to and including Ramesses II himself. Even in their complete state, however, several names would have been deliberately missing from the carvings. Those not listed were rulers apparently deemed too unfit to be remembered. Such 'kings lists' provide a valuable insight into the way in which ancient Egyptians chose to record their own history, and what each dynasty thought of its predecessors.

Listed below are ten names, nine of which appear on Ramesses II's king list. Place nine of these names into the grid opposite, one letter per box, until you are left with a single name that does not fit. This name belongs to a pharaoh who was not considered eligible for the list of kings. Can you guess why?

4 letters
SETI

6 letters
AHMOSE

8 letters
HOREMHAB
RAMESSES
THUTMOSE

9 letters
AMENEMHAT
AMENHOTEP
SENWOSRET

10 letters
MENTUHOTEP
HATSHEPSUT

Remaining pharaoh:

_____

Part of a limestone 'king list' featuring the names of thirty-four rulers.

16. Ancient Problems

The papyrus shown opposite, known as the Rhind Mathematical Papyrus, is an ancient Egyptian document that details dozens of number and geometry problems. It is most likely a mathematics textbook, for use by scribes in learning to solve particular mathematical problems via relevant examples.

Use your own mathematical skills to uncover more details about the papyrus. On each line below, apply the operations in turn from left to right until you reach the final box. Write your resulting solution into the empty box, to reveal the answer to the written description for each puzzle. As an added challenge, try to do each of these calculations in your head without written notes, if you can.

1. Approximation of pi, as calculated on the papyrus

10	× 15	+178	− 12	÷100	

2. Year in which the papyrus was written: _____ BCE

12	× 5	× 5	+ 10	× 5	

3. Number of mathematical problems explored on the papyrus

14	× 4	− 6	× 2	− 16	

4. Approximate length of an Egyptian royal cubit in centimetres

16	x 5	÷ 8	× 5	+ 2	

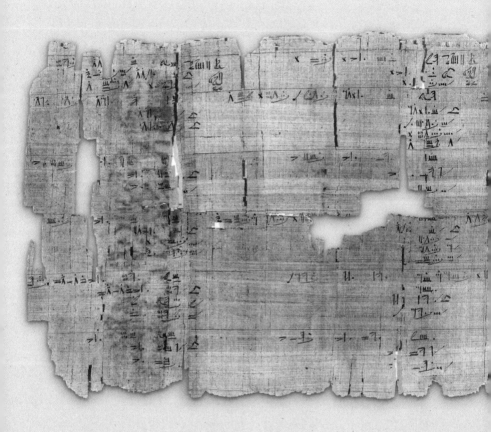

Detail of the Rhind Mathematical Papyrus. Compiled by Ahmose, an Egyptian scribe, the papyrus is thought to have been found during excavations near the Ramesseum in Egypt.

17. Ancient Games

The game counters pictured opposite date from the 1st century CE and feature numbers inscribed in both Greek and Roman scripts. Today, we primarily use Arabic numerals, with Roman numerals relegated to specific locations and contexts, such as on clock faces, building inscriptions and in the names of monarchs – as well as in some film and TV credits. Meanwhile, in modern Greece, Greek numerals are often used in similar situations to those in which other European countries use Roman numerals.

See how well you can play a game with Roman numerals, by completing the sudoku puzzle below. Simply place a number from I to VI into every empty square, so that no number repeats in any row, column or bold-lined 3×2 box.

IV					I
	I				
	V	I	VI		
	IV	VI	V		
			II		
VI					III

Made of rock crystal, these Roman game counters measure between 1.9 and 2.3 cm in diameter.

18. Picture This

The lintel shown opposite was carved in the 8th century CE, and is one of a collection found in the ancient Maya city of Yaxchilan, in modern-day Mexico. The image depicts an ancient ritual involving bloodletting. Along the top of the carving is a description in Maya script, although this particular example has been engraved as though seen in a mirror – for reasons unknown. Maya script uses a combination of pictorial logograms and syllabic glyphs to indicate both the meaning and the sounds of its language. At present, it is the best-deciphered Mesoamerican script, providing valuable insight into Maya culture.

Decipher the clues below to reveal four words associated with Maya culture. Each numbered clue can be solved to give exactly one word, with each clue combining both letters and images. For example, the letter 'E' with a picture of a seabird could be read as E + GULL = EAGLE.

1.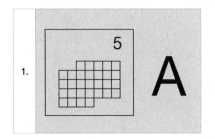

2.

3.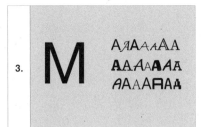

4.

The building from which this lintel was taken is dedicated to Shield Jaguar II's wife, Lady K'ab'al Xook, shown on the bottom right of the panel, conjuring a vision of a Teotihuacan serpent.

6

Treasures

The Museum's collection is one of the world's finest, with treasures from prehistoric times to the present day, and from cultures around the globe. Highlights include the Hoxne Hoard, a remarkable assemblage of gold and silver objects from Roman Britain; the Royal Gold Cup, made in the 14th century for French royalty; and the Olduvai stone chopping tool, more than a million years old.

The Museum also manages the nation's Portable Antiquities Scheme, which encourages the recording of archaeological objects found by members of the public in England and Wales. Some finds are designated Treasure as defined by the Treasure Act 1996 – whereby single finds of gold and silver over 300 years old, and groups or hoards of coins and prehistoric metalwork, must be declared in the public interest.

1. The Palmerston Cups

These cups, produced in about 1700, were used for drinking hot chocolate, a relatively new phenomenon in Europe at the time. Notably, the cups are made from the gold of mourning rings, which may have carried messages of remembrance for deceased relatives; they are also inscribed with messages encouraging the drinkers to remember their beloved dead – as well as their own mortality.

Uncover approximate translations of these cups' four inscriptions, below, by changing one letter in each word shown. No letters have been rearranged.

WE WAS NOW RESERVED SWEAT
UNCESS HI HIS WASTED BUTTER

SACKED SO SHE DEPORTED

THANK IN HOUR FRIANDS & DEPTH AT TIE THIEF

LIT AS BRINK NO TOE DEAR

The Palmerston Cups were made in London by John Chartier.

2. The Lycurgus Cup

The Lycurgus Cup, shown opposite, was made in the 4th century CE. Although the glass vessel's intricately cut detailing alone makes it worthy of admiration, it is most famous for another reason: it can change colour. When light shines through the glass and into the eye of the beholder, the glass appears red; when light shines directly on to it, however, an observer looking at it from the same side as the light source will see green. This type of glass is known as dichroic glass, and very few Roman examples survive.

Can you create a colour shift in each of the lines below by writing a regular English word at every step, progressing from left to right? Each word must use the same letters in the same order as the previous word, except with a single letter changed. For example, RED can become TAN like this: RED > FED > FAD > FAN > TAN.

| GOLD | > | > | > | SAGE |

| NAVY | > | > | > | PINK |

| BUFF | > | > | > | > | LIME |

| CYAN | > | > | > | > | PLUM |

The Lycurgus Cup is covered with various scenes representing the death of
Lycurgus, a king from Greek mythology famous for his persecution of Dionysus.

3. Medal Collection

Adorned with the faces of English and British rulers, these medals were all made by the Swiss engraver Jean Dassier in the 18th century. Medal sets such as this one, in the style of Roman coins commemorating a succession of emperors, were intended for collectors. The medals shown here were all struck in 1731, meaning the sequence ends with George II. A collection of such medals was donated to the British Museum by George IV, his grandson.

Try to arrange the medals into chronological order of reign, ending with the most recent ruler. When arranged in chronological order, the letters next to each medal will spell out a three-word phrase illegally stamped on to the reverse of the one-penny coin shown opposite, as a mark of protest.

1. GEORGE II – N	2. WILLIAM II – O
3. OLIVER CROMWELL – O	4. EDWARD VI – O
5. ANNE – E	6. RICHARD II – T

7. HENRY IV – E

8. WILLIAM I – V

9. WILLIAM III – M

10. ELIZABETH I – W

11. HENRY VIII – F

12. MARY I – R

13. RICHARD III – S

Stamped phrase:

_____   _____

4. The Hoxne Hoard

Together with the rings pictured above it, the gold bracelet shown opposite was found in Suffolk in 1992 and forms part of a collection of found Roman treasure known as the Hoxne Hoard. Consisting of both silver and gold items, the hoard is the largest of its kind discovered in Britain. The intricate design on the bracelet was evidently made in part by punching holes through the metal. A message can be read around these holes.

Draw a loop through all of the white squares in the grid below, avoiding the shaded holes in the grid, to reveal the bracelet's message. The loop can visit each square only once, and must move horizontally or vertically between squares. Once the loop has been completed, a translation of the message carved around the punched-out holes of the bracelet will be revealed by reading the letters in clockwise order along the loop, starting from the 'U' at the top-left corner.

							E		
U			S			I			
	P	A		S					
									T
A	P		H			H			
			I		Y				
	N			L				D	
									Y
A				L	L		A		
		I			U			J	

In addition to these items of jewellery, the Hoxne Hoard includes approximately 15,000 coins. The objects were probably buried for safety at a time when Britain was passing out of Roman control.

5. The Thetford Hoard 1

Containing a mixture of gold and silver items, the Thetford
Hoard was discovered in Norfolk in 1979. Several of the found
items include references to pagan gods and practices, despite
being buried in 4th-century Roman Britain – which was officially
Christian at the time. The artefact pictured opposite is an ornate
belt buckle found with the hoard, with two delicately carved horses
on the loop and a larger plate featuring an image of a pagan satyr.

Can you 'unbuckle' the two types of treasure on each line below to
reveal a catalogue of the items that were found in Thetford? All of
the letters on each line remain in the correct order for each item but
have been interleaved in some way. **C*PIO*N*IN***, for example, can be
unbuckled to give COIN and PIN. The numbers to the left and right
of each line reveal how many of each item were found, with numbers
on the left matching the item that starts with the leftmost letter, and
those on the right matching the count of the other item.

Treasure: Treasure:

1 x _____   GBEOXM   _____ 1 x

3 x _____   BRIENAGD   _____ 22 x

4 x _____   BNERCAKCLEALCETE   _____ 5 x

4 x _____   PAMEUNLDEATNT   _____ 1 x

3 x _____   STSRPAOIONENR   _____ 33 x

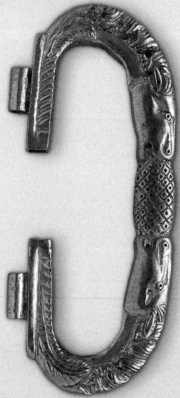

The satyr featured on the buckle is part of
a Bacchic theme that links the buckle with
certain other items among the hoard.

6. The Thetford Hoard 2

Pictured to the right is one of the many items of jewellery found in the Thetford Hoard. It is thought that the treasures may have been made for sale but never bought, and therefore never used or worn in Roman times. This may explain why some of them show very little sign of wear, such as this gold ring with several precious gems set into it.

In the stylized representation of the ring directly below, some letters have been added in place of the gems. Try to find a relevant word that uses all of the letters exactly once.

Then, have a go at finding further words that each use the centre letter ('A') plus two or more of the other letters. No letter may be used within a word more times than it occurs on the ring. How many words can you find? There are at least fifty to discover.

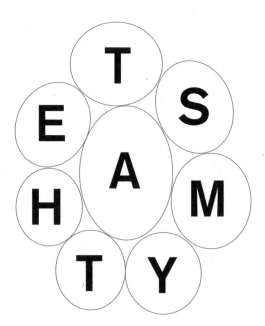

7. Ædwen's Brooch

The silver brooch shown below was probably made in the 11th century, and has an intricately carved design on the front featuring several animals that may be mythical in nature. Thanks to an Old English inscription on the back of the brooch, it is believed to have belonged to a woman of considerable social standing known as Ædwen. Are you able to solve the puzzle below to reveal part of the message on the reverse?

Each of the lines below has a partially obscured central word, which can be added to the end of the first word and the beginning of the second word to form two new words. For example, GRID and SMITH could have the word LOCK in their centre, forming GRIDLOCK and LOCKSMITH. The six concealed words reveal, when read from top to bottom, the first line of the inscription on the back of the brooch that follows immediately on from 'Ædwen owns …'. Some letters have been given already to help you – add in one letter per underline to complete the missing words.

CHI   M _   DIAL

DIS   _ _ Y   BE

SEE   _ H _   REIN

WAR   _ O _ _   SHIP

TUMBLED   _ W _   SOME

RAT   _ _ R   RING

8. The Royal Gold Cup

The Royal Gold Cup, pictured opposite, was made in Paris in the 14th century for the French royal family. As its name suggests, the cup itself is made from solid gold, while the outer edges are decorated with intricately enamelled scenes depicting the martyrdom of a Christian saint.

Use your solving skills to uncover more information about this majestic artefact. Mentally rotate each of the various discs opposite until six words relating to the Royal Gold Cup each line up simultaneously, reading out from the centre. These six words then provide the answers to the six clues below.

- Medieval saint depicted in enamel: _____

- Precious gemstone used for embellishment: _____

- Stylized rose type depicted on the stem: _____

- Language of the inscription: _____

- Country where the cup spent 300 years: _____

- '_____-taille', enamelling technique: _____

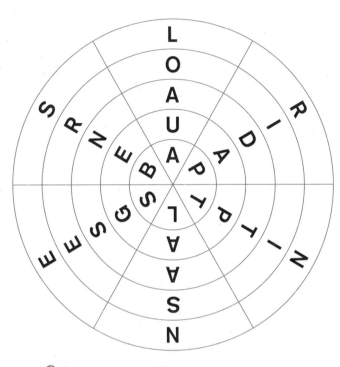

9. The Hedwig Beakers

The glass below is one of the known 'Hedwig Beakers', named after a European saint once thought to own a set. According to legend, when St Hedwig drank water from one of her glasses, it miraculously turned into wine. Glasses made in the same style and series as St Hedwig's then became highly prized items, considered a type of religious relic.

Only one Hedwig beaker resides in the British Museum, but several others are on display in museums across Europe, and one in New York. Some beakers have also been hidden in the grid opposite, and can be revealed using the number clues. Each number reveals the total number of beakers hiding in the squares touching it – including diagonally. No more than one beaker is hidden per square, however, and no beakers can be found in the numbered squares. Mark in the locations of all the hidden beakers; once you have located them all, the number of beakers you have revealed will be equal to the total number of known, complete Hedwig beakers.

	1			2		1
3	3	3	2		2	
		2				
			3	2	2	
2						1
	2		4	4		1
1	1	1			2	

Number of complete
Hedwig beakers:

_____

Opposite: This Hedwig Beaker is thought
to have been made in the East Mediterranean
or Sicily around 1150–1220.

10. The Jewels of Ur

Situated in modern-day Iraq, the Royal Tomb of Ur was first excavated in 1922. Magnificent headdresses, personal ornaments and items of jewellery were found buried alongside the noble inhabitants of the cemetery – most notable of whom was the queen Puabi. The jewels shown on these pages are just some of the vast collection found at Ur, many of which involve intricate beadwork and precious materials.

String together each of the lettered beads below, to spell out the names of five materials used in the making of the jewellery found at Ur. All of the beads are used exactly once, and four of the resulting materials are one word long while the other is composed of two words.

AGA   AN   AZ   CA   ELI   GO   ER   LAP   LV   ISL   LD   RN   SI   TE   ULI

Materials:

_____

_____

_____

_____

_____

Just some of the many items
of jewellery found at the Royal
Tomb of Ur, excavated by
Sir Leonard Woolley.

11. The Qianlong Bi

Bi, such as the one shown below, are generally unadorned ceremonial discs carved from jade, and were associated with the heavens in ancient Chinese cultures. This particular jade *bi* may have been created as early as 1200 BCE, but the inscription was added around 3,000 years later, in 1790 CE. The Chinese emperor at the time, Qianlong, wrote a poem that he ordered to be inscribed on the ancient artefact, the lyrics of which he believed explained the provenance and function of *bi*.

Find a route through the *bi* maze opposite, revealing as you journey what the emperor believed these artefacts were used for. In particular, you must travel from the entrance at the top of the maze to the exit at the bottom without retracing your steps. The correct route will pass over, in order, letters that spell out two words that form the crux of the emperor's poem.

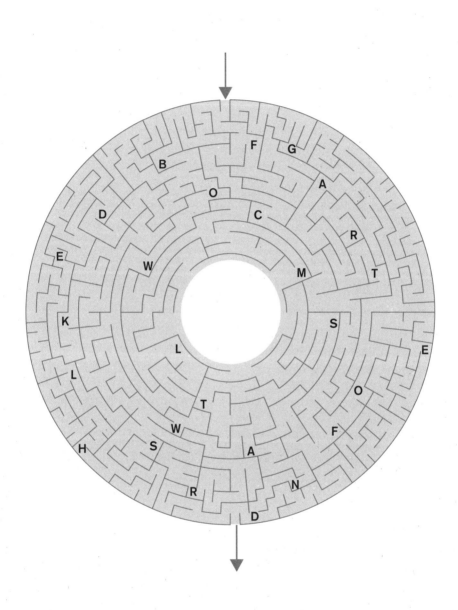

Key poem words:

_____   _____

12. The Mold Cape

The cape shown below was discovered in Mold, Wales, and remains one of the most ornate examples of prehistoric sheet-metal working ever found. It may have been made as early as 1900 BCE and used with ceremonial or religious purpose. It is believed to have been made from a single gold ingot, beaten thin and then decorated with an intricate pattern of dots resembling strings of beads and gems. Although the cape had been badly crushed by the time of its discovery, it has since been meticulously restored by matching up many small fragments of the dotted metal.

The Mold Cape (top left) with details showing the intricate nature of its decoration.

Piece together an intricate design of your own below, based on the numbered fragments you have been given. Join the circled numbers with horizontal or vertical lines, where each number must have as many lines connected to it as specified by its value. No more than two lines may join any given pair of numbers, and no lines may cross either each other or another circle. The finished layout must also connect all circles, so you can travel between any pair of numbers by following one or more lines.

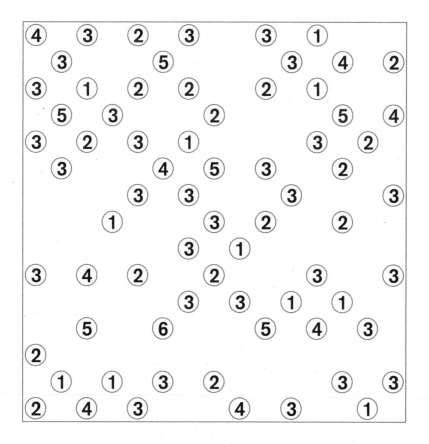

13. The Olduvai Stone Chopping Tool

The stone tool shown at the bottom of this page is 1.2 million years old, making it one of the oldest artefacts in the British Museum.

In the explanatory text below, several key words have had some letters 'chopped out'. Can you fill in the gaps, with one letter per gap, to reveal more information about this ancient artefact?

- The stone used is B _ S _ L _ , a volcanic rock

- The cutting edge was made with another, harder stone, used as a _ A _ M _ R

- This stone was uncovered in the country now known as T _ N _ A _ I _

- A series of _ A _ T _ Q _ A _ E _ has gradually exposed buried artefacts in the region

- It may have been used for obtaining B _ N _ M _ R _ O _ , an essential food source

- The tools were likely made by a _ U _ A _ species similar to our own

- Tools of this kind are the earliest examples of _ E _ H _ O _ O _ Y

Solutions

1 The British Museum

1. Who's Who?

From left to right, the human figures depict the following:

1. UNCIVILIZED MAN
2. ANGEL
3. HUNTER
4. FARMER
5. ARCHITECTURE
6. SCULPTURE
7. PAINTING
8. SCIENCE
9. MATHEMATICS
10. DRAMA
11. POETRY
12. MUSIC
13. CIVILIZED MAN

2. Glass Ceiling

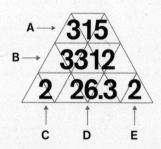

Therefore,

- **315** = total weight of the glass panels, in tonnes
- **3312** = number of triangular panels on the roof
- **2** = size of the inner courtyard in acres
- **26.3** = greatest height of the roof in metres
- **2** = number of weeks needed to clean the roof

3. Reading Maze

The Reading Room therefore opened on 02/05/1857, i.e. 2 May 1857.

4. Match the '-ology'

1. Conchology, study of mollusc shells – D
2. Vexillology, study of flags – C
3. Deltiology, study of postcards – B
4. Campanology, study of bells – A
5. Oology, study of eggs – F
6. Balneology, study of bathing – E

5. An Unusual Discovery

The object is a pair of SPECTACLES. It is believed that they may have
accidentally fallen into the sarcophagus when it was opened at the turn of
the 20th century, and thus lay concealed inside until its reopening in 1988.

The words clued by the pictures are:

A. PESTLE
B. CLASP
C. PESETA (or PESETAS)
D. PLEATS
E. PETALS
F. TASSEL

Additional words to find include:

accepts, access, aces, acts, ales, apes, apse, apses, asleep, asp, aspect,
aspects, asps, ass, asset, ates, capes, caplets, caps, case, cases, cast, caste,
castes, castle, castles, casts, cats, cease, ceases, celesta, celestas, claps,
clasps, class, cleats, ease, easel, easels, eases, east, eats, eels, elapse, elapses,
elects, else, escape, escapes, laces, laps, lapse, lapses, lass, last, lasts, lats,
leaps, leas, lease, leases, least, lees, less, lest, lets, paces, pacts, pales, palest,
pals, pas, pass, passe, past, paste, pastel, pastels, pastes, pasts, pates, pats,
peals, peas, peels, pelts, pest, pestles, pests, pets, places, plates, pleas, please,
pleases, psst, sac, sacs, sale, sales, salt, salts, sap, saps, sat, sate, sates, scale,
scales, scalp, scalps, sea, seal, seals, seas, seat, seats, sect, sects, see, seep,
seeps, sees, select, selects, sepal, sepals, septa, set, sets, slap, slaps, slat, slate,
slates, slats, sleep, sleeps, sleet, sleets, slept, spa, space, spaces, spas, spat,
spate, spats, spec, specs, spectacle, spelt, splat, stale, stales, staple, staples,
steal, steals, steel, steels, steep, steeps, step, steps, taels, tales, tapes, taps,
teals, teas, tease, teasel, teasels, teases and tees.

6. Cats' Tales

B	J	K	T	C	S	L	E	A
T	L	E	K	J	A	C	B	S
C	S	A	L	B	E	K	T	J
K	B	S	C	L	T	J	A	E
J	E	T	A	K	B	S	L	C
A	C	L	E	S	J	T	K	B
L	K	J	B	E	C	A	S	T
S	A	B	J	T	K	E	C	L
E	T	C	S	A	L	B	J	K

The name of the cat responsible for bringing Mike to the Museum's attention was BLACK JACK.

7. Rainbow Railings

The name of the colour on the railings is therefore INVISIBLE GREEN.

8. Discus: Discuss

All of the Greek words have had their head letter reflected to face the wrong way, and as such their 'heads' are all 'facing the wrong way'. The Townley statue shown on the puzzle page similarly has its head facing the wrong way, after it was incorrectly restored. The other extant copies consistently show the thrower looking back towards his discus.

9. True or False?

1.   The British Museum and the United States of America were founded in the same year – FALSE: The British Museum is 17 years older than the USA
2.   The British Museum introduced electric lighting in 1879 – TRUE
3.   A snail, glued to a card and exhibited in the British Museum, was found to be alive after four years of being on display – TRUE
4.   'Marbles' is the most-searched term on the British Museum website – FALSE: it's 'Egypt'
5.   During both World Wars, the Museum evacuated some of its artefacts and exhibitions to Wales, in case of attack – TRUE
6.   The street artist Banksy spray-painted an image of a mouse on to a Museum wall in 2005 – FALSE, although he did sneak in an 'artefact': a rock he had painted to feature a caveman and a shopping trolley
7.   The British Museum once had its own London Underground station – TRUE
8.   The film *Vertigo*, directed by Alfred Hitchcock, was partly filmed at the British Museum – FALSE: though his film Blackmail was partly shot there
9.   A young W. A. Mozart visited the British Museum on an outing with his family shortly after it opened – TRUE
10. The main entrance to the British Museum is on Bloomsbury Street, London – FALSE: It's on Great Russell Street

2 Everyday Living

1. The Cities that Were

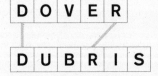

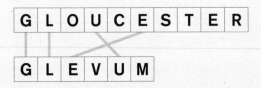

The modern-day city where the tombstones were located is therefore Lincoln.

2. Fun and Games

	C	M	E	H	C	H
E	H	I	R	E	A	I
S	E	N	A	N	P	S
S	S	E	W	G	N	I
O	G	T	D	I	O	U
R	U	S	E	C	J	R
O	K	U	M	A	H	

1. CHESS – B
2. SENET – E
3. DICE – D
4. SUGOROKU – I
5. MAHJONG – A
6. WARI – F
7. MEHEN – H
8. PACHISI – C
9. UR – G

3. The Lewis Chessmen

The letters in the shaded squares can be rearranged to reveal HARRY POTTER. Animated versions of the chessmen can be seen in the first film of the franchise, in a scene where the pieces come alive during a game.

4. Everyday A-maze-ing

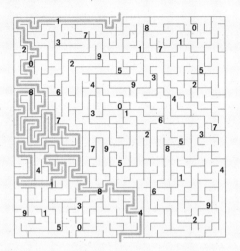

The following numbers are crossed over in turn: 1, 0, 8, 1, 8 and 4. As of 2022, there are 108,184 Greek artefacts held by the British Museum, of which almost 6,500 are on display.

5. Undiluted Beauty

The artist's inscription therefore reads SOPHILOS PAINTED ME.

6. Complaining for Ages

'When you came, you said to me as follows: "I will give Gimil-Sin (when he
COMES) FINE quality COPPER ingots." You LEFT then but you did not do
what you PROMISED me. You PUT ingots that were not GOOD before my
messenger (Sit-Sin) and SAID: "If you want to TAKE them, TAKE them; if you
do not want to TAKE them, go away!" What do you TAKE me for, that you
TREAT somebody like me with SUCH contempt … Take cognisance that
(from NOW on) I will not ACCEPT here any COPPER from you that is not
of FINE quality. I shall (from NOW on) select and TAKE the ingots individually
in my own YARD, and I SHALL exercise against you my RIGHT of REJECTION
because you have TREATED me with contempt.'

7. Keeping Track

- BEAR: The calendar was designed for riders to inscri**be a r**ecord of their
  hunts over the course of a year

- DEER: Red wax strips provi**de er**asable – and reusable – areas for
  marking the time and date of successful pursuits

- HARE: The German names for each mont**h are** shown on the right-hand
  side of the calendar, as can be seen in the lower image opposite

- WOLF: Hunting dogs of different breeds, each noted for their accurate,
  narro**w olf**action, are also illustrated

- CALF: Medieval hunters may have travelled long distances in pursuit
  of their quarry, staying with lo**cal f**amilies and landed gentry

8. Cups and Saucers

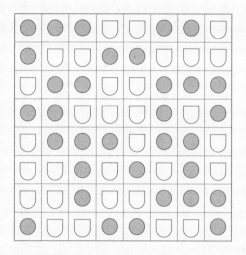

9. Hadrian's Wall

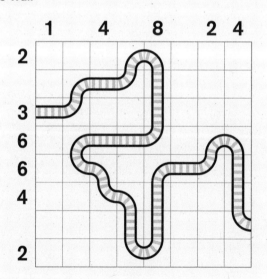

Hadrian's approximate age was therefore 30.

10. Glass Fragments

The text refers to the Museum's restoration of eight glass vessels after [an] explosion in Beirut, Lebanon. Working with the Archaeological Museum at the American University of Beirut, conservators from the British Museum meticulously restored the objects that had been shattered by the impact, extricating the fragments from the also-destroyed windows and display cases.

11. Finding the Way

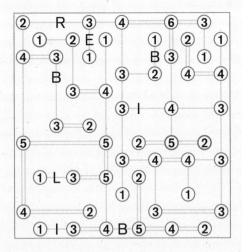

Reading from left to right, top to bottom, the crossed letters reveal that a shell and cane chart is known as a REBBILIB.

12. Loop the Loop

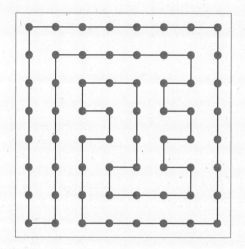

13. Musical Marvel

The horizontal lines represent letters, from 'A' on the bottom line to 'Y' on the top line, with the rest of the alphabet spaced evenly between. The placement of the notes indicates which letters to read, from left to right, as follows:

The instrument features the coat of arms of Queen Elizabeth I.

14. A Load of Old Rubbish

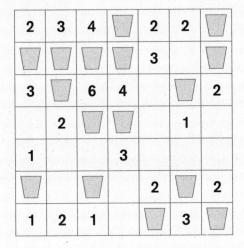

There are 16 buried cups – so the disposable clay cup was made around the year 1600 BCE.

15. Age-Old Eats

BREAD – D
COOKIE – C
DUCK – B
FIGS – E
FISH – A
PASTRY – F

The historian is Mary BEARD – whose surname is an anagram of BREAD. The three-cornered loaf of bread (image D) is believed to be the one that inspired her on her first visit to the Museum.

3 The Animal Kingdom

1. Colossal Animals

1.   HORSE – C

2.   LION – A

3.   SCARAB – B

2. Immortal Animals 1

1.   OWL + JADE: C
2.   BIRD + LAPIS: E
3.   CAT + BRONZE: G
4.   LION + GYPSUM: B
5.   CAMEL + PLASTER: F
6.   TERRAPIN + NEPHRITE: A
7.   HIPPOPOTAMUS + TERRACOTTA: D

3. Encoded Animals

The encoded animals are:

- COBRA (DPCSB, 3-15-2-18-1, OCRBA, CUBRE)
- GECKO (HFDLP, 7-5-3-11-15, EGKCO, GICKU)
- IBEX (JCFY, 9-2-5-24, BIXE, OBIX)
- IBIS (JCJT, 9-2-9-19, BISI, OBOS)
- JACKAL (KBDLBM, 10-1-3-11-1-12, AJKCLA, JECKEL)
- ORYX (PSZY, 15-18-25-24, ROXY, URYX)
- TILAPIA (UJMBQJB, 20-9-12-1-16-9-1, ITALIPA, TOLEPOE)
- VULTURE (WVMUVSF, 22-21-12-20-21-18-5, UVTLRUE, VALTARI)

The codes are as follows:

- List 1: All letters have been shifted forward one place in the alphabet (A to B, B to C, C to D and so on through until Y to Z and Z to A)
- List 2: All letters have been replaced with numbers: A with 1, B with 2, C with 3, and so on
- List 3: Consecutive letter pairs have been swapped
- List 4: All vowels have been shifted forward one place in the alphabet (A to E, E to I, I to O, O to U and U to A)

In addition, when each secret word is decoded, then read in the order of its list from 1 to 4, the following message is revealed: OPEN THE TOMB QUIETLY.

4. In the Labyrinth

The mythical creatures, in the order visited, are:

- MERMAID
- PHOENIX
- SPHINX
- SIREN
- GRIFFIN
- UNICORN
- MINOTAUR – which is therefore the creature nearest the centre of the labyrinth

A	I	D	P	H	O
M	M	N	I	S	X	E
E	R	X	H	P	I	N
R	I	S		A	T	O
E	N	G	R	U	I	N
F	I	R	N	I	M	N
F	I	N	U	C	O	R

5. Sacred Animal Pairs

1. ZEUS + BULL: E
2. APOLLO + CICADA: A
3. ARES + BOAR: F
4. DEMETER + SERPENT: B
5. HESTIA + DONKEY: D
6. RHEA + LION: C

6. Hunting the Hunted

Z	K	I	E	A	S	R	E	E	D	L	R	H
E	Z	H	R	H	I	A	C	R	A	T	A	N
N	E	R	A	R	R	S	A	S	A	R	H	B
O	G	R	K	D	T	R	H	L	T	I	I	A
S	E	E	S	B	S	A	R	E	N	E	B	O
T	H	O	L	R	A	B	B	Z	C	R	O	E
R	T	R	T	L	E	E	R	R	A	R	A	A
I	T	R	C	I	E	B	A	C	O	E	R	G
C	Z	T	H	S	S	Z	E	A	A	R	E	T
H	I	C	T	C	L	G	A	A	R	R	L	A
B	E	I	C	A	L	Z	B	G	J	I	H	A
J	A	C	K	A	L	A	O	I	O	Z	A	C
R	A	L	R	R	R	L	H	N	L	K	E	I

The animals, in the order listed, are:

- BOAR
- DEER
- HARE
- LION
- JACKAL
- GAZELLE
- OSTRICH
- HARTEBEEST

The only one of these not to appear on the artefact is the BOAR.

7. Therianthropic Theory

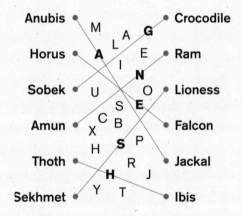

The crossed letters spell GANESH, a Hindu deity depicted with the head of an elephant.

8. Immortal Animals 2

1. DOG + CLAY: B
2. BULL + COPPER: F
3. CATFISH + IRON: E
4. COW + CALCITE: G
5. TIGER + MARBLE: C

6.   TURTLE + STONE: A
7.   BUTTERFLY + TORTOISESHELL: D

9. Start and End

The animals are:

A.   Dachshund
B.   Rooster
C.   Alpaca
D.   Groundhog
E.   Eagle
F.   Reindeer

10. The Four Sons of Horus

From left to right in the image, the Sons and their affiliations are:

- Qebehsenuef: he has a falcon's head and protects the intestines
- Hapy: he has a baboon's head and protects the lungs
- Imsety: he has a human head and protects the liver
- Duamutef: he has a jackal's head and protects the stomach

11. Cat Caption Competition

1.   THE LARGE CAT – D
2.   ALICE AND THE CHESHIRE CAT – C
3.   CAT LOOKING AT RICE FIELDS NEAR ASAKUSA – B
4.   HORRIBLE END OF A GOLDFISH – A

12. Go Fish

1.   Three – two adults and a child
2.   It has legs, and seems to be walking
3.   A crab and a lobster

4. Two
5. C.
6. Ecce

13. What's In A Name?

In the order listed, the names are:

- ENEMY CATCHER
- ENEMY BITER
- LOUD BARKER
- REMOVER OF EVIL
- DON'T THINK, BITE

14. Fishy Floor

The sea creatures are:

- BREAM
- COMBER
- DENTEX
- MULLET
- SEA BASS
- OCTOPUS
- MORAY EEL
- GREEN WRASSE
- SPINY LOBSTER
- SCORPIONFISH
- RAINBOW WRASSE

15. Animal Amulets

16. Best Friends

- 2000–1700 BCE, Crete, Greece – E
- 1350–1300 BCE, Thebes, Egypt – B
- 600–580 BCE, Boeotia, Greece – C
- 1st century BCE–2nd century CE, Egypt – F
- 300 BCE–300 CE, Mexico – G
- 150–50 BCE, Hounslow, England – H
- 1st or 2nd century CE, China – A
- 1st or 2nd century CE, Italy – D

17. Lion Hunts

```
I L O L O I L I N N O I N
N N L L I I N N N L N N I
I L I O I O N O L O O I O
L L L L O O O N L I L I N
N L I O L O L L N N N L I
L O I O I I O N O I L O I
O N O I I L O I N L I O O
O I I O L L I L L L L I O
L O I N O O L I I O N O I
N O O L N O O I N L I N I
O L I O O O L O N N N N I
O O I L N O N O I N O L L
I N I I O L L I L L L N N
```

18. Intoxicating Animals

1.   BEAR + WINE – C
2.   STAG + BEER – E
3.   UNICORN + MARSALA – F
4.   BOAR + MEAD – B
5.   DRAGON + BRANDY – A
6.   COCKEREL + VERMOUTH – D

19. Shape Shifters

Possible solutions are:

1.

| EEL | GEL | GET | MET | MEN | MAN |

2.

| CRAB | CRAG | BRAG | BRAS | BOAS | BOYS |

3.

| SHARK | SHANK | THANK | THINK | THINS | TWINS |

4.

| BASS | LASS | LESS | LENS | LENT | GENT |

20. Unusual Figures

1.   RATTLESNAKE - D
2.   WOLVERINE - B
3.   WALRUS - E
4.   CUTTLEFISH - F
5.   KILLER WHALE - A
6.   ARMADILLO - C

4 Myth and Magic

1. Missing Mosaic

1. TURQUOISE
2. CONCH SHELL
3. PYRITE
4. DEER SKIN
5. LIGNITE
6. PINE
7. AGAVE

The remaining letters spell DEITY.

2. Sarcophagus Stack

Their names are:

- PAKAP

```
P _ _ _ P
 A _ A
  K
```

- NEBAMUN

```
N _ _ _ _ _ N
 E _ _ _ U
  B _ M
   A
```

- SASOBEK

```
S _ _ _ _ _ K
 A _ _ _ E
  S _ B
   O
```

- MERYMOSE

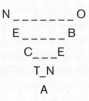

```
M _ _ _ _ _ _ E
  E _ _ _ _ S
    R _ _ O
      YM
```

- NECTANEBO

```
N _ _ _ _ _ _ _ O
  E _ _ _ _ _ B
    C _ _ _ E
      T_N
        A
```

3. Totem Tales

T – There was once a village whose people lost their fishhooks each time they fished

H – The fishhooks – with fish attached – were being taken by the creator figure Yetl

U – Yetl usually took the form of a raven, but was currently swimming in the water and taking fish for himself

N – To try and capture the thief, the villagers began to make two-pronged fishhooks

D – The villagers baited their new hooks with devil fish and lowered them into the water

E – Yetl took the bait, and the villagers battled to reel in their catch

R – They finally pulled the hook from the water, which had part of Yetl's raven beak attached

B – Without his beak, Yetl transformed into human form and hid his damaged face

I – He persuaded the villagers, who accepted him as a guest, to give back his beak

R – With his beak returned, Yetl then reappeared to the villagers in the form of a wise human chief, and ate with the villagers

D – The final figure of Yetl as the wise chief is represented at the top of the totem pole

The creature found on many totem poles is therefore a THUNDERBIRD.

4. Totem Tales Too

B	E	A	R		
B	E	A	V	E	R
E	A	G	L	E	
F	I	S	H		
F	R	O	G		
R	A	V	E	N	
S	A	L	M	O	N
W	H	A	L	E	
W	O	L	F		

5. Evil Eyes Everywhere

2	●	●	●	2	●	
3	●	7	4		1	
3	●	●	●	1		1
2	●		2		2	●
	3	2		2		●
●		●	2	●	●	2
1	2			2	2	

6. The National God of Rurutu

- The figure is thought to be made of SANDALWOOD
- The figure's FEET and lower legs are missing
- The statue is HOLLOW at the back and features a removeable lid
- The cavity may have been used to store the SKULL or bones of a significant ancestor
- When used, the figure may then have been WRAPPED with feathered cord
- The statue may have been polished with coconut oil and cowrie SHELLS
- The statue was taken by MISSIONARIES and brought to London
- The statue has travelled to various cities on exhibition, including Paris and CANBERRA
- The statue has been copied many times: the artist PICASSO owned a version

The god depicted by the statue is A'a: supreme deity of the island of Rurutu.

7. Incantation Bowl

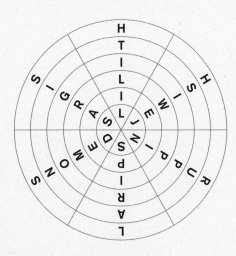

LILITH: Biblical figure cited as the first wife of Adam, banished from Eden and considered an evil spirit

JEWISH: Dialect of Babylonian Aramaic found on most incantation bowls

NIPPUR: Sumerian city where multiple bowls were found buried

SPIRAL: Shape in which most incantations were written

DEMONS: Malevolent spirits from whom incantation bowls offered protection

SARGIS: Name of the beneficiary inscribed on the bowl shown here

8. Omnipresent Goddesses

1.   SATIS: Egyptian goddess of the flood – D
2.   ANAHITA: Iranian water goddess – G
3.   SPES: Roman goddess of hope – I
4.   ATHENA: Greek goddess of wisdom – A
5.   TANIT: Punic goddess of Carthage – B
6.   UTTU: Mesopotamian goddess associated with weaving and spiders – H
7.   IZANAMI: Japanese goddess of creation – C
8.   DRYAD: One of several tree nymphs in Greek mythology – F
9.   TAWERET: Egyptian goddess of childbirth – E

9. Dr Dee's Crystal Ball

ANGEL
AZTEC
ELIZABETH
KRAKOW
OBSIDIAN

10. Day of the Dead 1

The name of the female figure is Catrina, also known as La Catrina.

11. Day of the Dead 2

MEXICO   Country associated with the Day of the Dead
NOVEMBER   The month in which Día de los Muertos falls
CALAVERA   Spanish name for a traditional sugar skull
MEZCAL   Alcoholic spirit sometimes included in an *ofrenda*
CRUCIFIX   Catholic symbol sometimes included in an *ofrenda*
HIBISCUS   Exotic flower from which traditional tea is made
SKELETON   Shape of traditional *calacas* figurines
ARIZONA   US state which holds a Day of the Dead procession

12. Hindu Deities

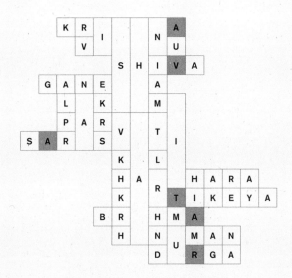

The revealed Sanskrit word is AVATAR.

13. Masked Meaning

JAPAN + DRAGON – C
ALASKA + RED FOX – D
CANADA + HAWK – A
NEW CALEDONIA + DECEASED CHIEF – E
CAROLINE ISLANDS + DEIFIED ANCESTOR – B

14. The Rivers of Eden

```
H G A E A A T R A H N C K D T
G T I P R I D I H D T E T O E
P E K C H T H T I K A L K O N
R T D L S I A E G G O S G T D
A G T T R L H A L S G A T O T
O E H P K G P S E D G O L A H
H D H I S G I S L I S L L O T
A H E N C D T C K E T E L R T
K O O H O O C T T A D K O L D
T D K O S H P D R R P E D A C
P G C R C T S E I N P D L A A
H C I A K H P I O L S I C G I
S G N H K A A E P H N H E H I
R D H T O G N O T C P C H N P
K I R E O N L S P D D O R O O
```

15. Fishy Tales

1. After angering the SNAKE goddess Manasa, a man was killed
   by SERPENTS. His wife, Behula, refused to CREMATE his
   body. Instead, she tried to bring him back to life by carrying him
   through a great RIVER. The husband's KNEE was then eaten by
   one of the fish. After appeasing the gods, it was agreed that Behula's
   husband could be RESURRECTED. This was done, but only
   after the KNEE was taken from the stomach of the fish who
   SWALLOWED it. – Image B

2. A man named Tametomo and his family were caught in a great
   STORM at sea, which is said to have been caused by a vengeful
   DRAGON. To appease the gods, his wife decided to SACRIFICE
   herself to the sea. Tametomo and his son found refuge on the back
   of a huge SHARK. They were saved by tengu – beings that are part
   BIRD and part HUMAN. – Image D

3. After a brief adventure on the MOON, a man named Lucian and his group return to EARTH. While swimming in a calm sea, they are swallowed by a WHALE. Inside the beast, they find TREES, birds and HERBS. The group kill the creature that swallowed them by starting a BONFIRE in its stomach. They manage to escape by PROPPING its mouth open. – Image A

4. As a young boy, the WARRIOR Benkei was known as Oniwaka. Whilst studying in a TEMPLE, Oniwaka discovered that a giant CARP had killed his mother. His mother had fallen off the edge of the large WATERFALL, and been killed in the POOL at the bottom. Onikawa used his extraordinary STRENGTH to kill the beast, and AVENGE his mother's death. – Image C

16. Gods of Chaos

The gods and civilizations can be matched as follows:

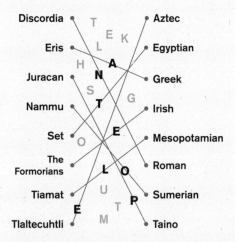

The ANTELOPE was considered to be a symbol of chaos by the ancient Egyptians.

17. Snake Link

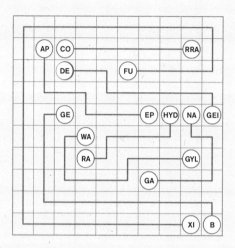

APEP – Egyptian god of death, embodied as a snake

CORRA – Serpent goddess in Irish mythology

DEGEI – supreme god of Fijian mythology and creator of Fijian islands

FUXI – Creation god in Chinese mythology, depicted with a snake's tail

GEB – Egyptian god of the earth, considered to be the father of snakes

HYDRA – Sea serpent in Greek mythology

NAGA – A name for part-human, part-serpent deities in Hinduism

WAGYL – Name for the Aboriginal Rainbow Serpent used by the
Noongar in Australia

18. Rings of Magic

1. This ring with a magical Old English runic inscription was found in CARLISLE – C
2. This ring with astrological symbols is inscribed with the names of the angels Sadayel, Tiriel and RAPHAEL – B
3. The underside of this Egyptian swivelling ring features a hidden image of a SCORPION – E
4. This brass warrior talisman ring is from the Indonesian island of SUMATRA – F
5. This bronze amulet ring is inscribed with the name of the angel ANAEL – H
6. This gold ring has a Latin inscription associated with EXORCISM – A
7. This amulet ring, which may have been used to protect against kidney disease, features a mythical TOADSTONE – G
8. This opal ring inscribed with charms also features images of two MONSTERS – D

19. Magic Squares of Mars

11	24	7	20	3
4	12	25	8	16
17	5	13	21	9
10	18	1	14	22
23	6	19	2	15

20. The Nasca Lines

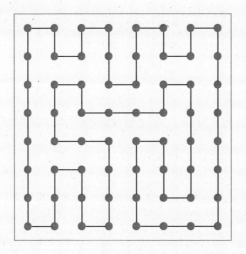

5 The Written Word

1. An Increasing Problem

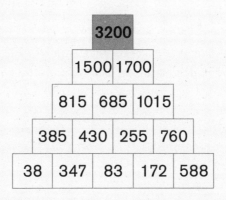

The plaster counting tablet was made in approximately 3200 BCE – meaning it is over 5,000 years old.

2. Un-written in Stone

The missing names are PRINCE GETA and EMPRESS PLAUTILLA. They were probably both killed on the orders of Antoninus Pius – known better as Caracalla – who was, respectively, their brother and husband.

3. The Handscroll of Admonitions

'To utter a word, how light a THING that seems! Yet from a word, both HONOUR and SHAME proceed. Do not think that that you are HIDDEN; For the DIVINE mirror REFLECTS even that which cannot be seen. Do not think that you have been NOISELESS; God's EAR needs no SOUND. Do not BOAST of your glory; For heaven's law HATES what is full. Do not put your TRUST in honours and high birth; For he that is HIGHEST falls. Make the 'Little STARS' your PATTERN. Do not let your FANCIES ROAM afar. Let your HEARTS be as the LOCUSTS And your RACE shall multiply.'

4. Alphabetical Zeal

1. ETRUSCAN – A
2. LATIN – D
3. HEBREW – E
4. RUNIC – B
5. GREEK – C

5. The Franks Casket

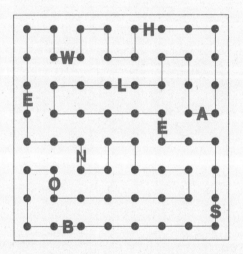

The crossed through-letters reveal that 'WHALESBONE' – i.e. whale's bone – was used to make the casket.

6. Reading the Runes

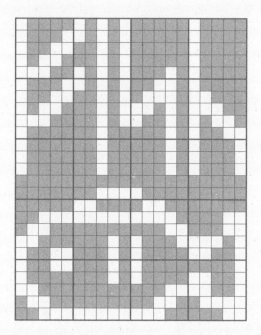

The runes spell FISH, as indicated by the image at the bottom of the grid.

7. The Epic Library

A	U	N	R	B	L	I	S	P	H	T	E
I	S	E	T	P	U	N	H	L	A	R	B
B	P	H	L	T	A	R	E	N	S	U	I
L	I	T	U	E	H	S	A	B	R	P	N
S	H	A	B	R	N	P	I	T	E	L	U
R	E	P	N	L	B	T	U	A	I	S	H
N	L	I	H	U	S	A	P	E	T	B	R
U	A	R	E	I	T	B	N	S	L	H	P
P	T	B	S	H	E	L	R	I	U	N	A
T	R	L	A	N	I	U	B	H	P	E	S
H	N	U	I	S	P	E	L	R	B	A	T
E	B	S	P	A	R	H	T	U	N	I	L

The library is named after ASHURBANIPAL, the last great king of the
Assyrian empire.

8. The Epic Poem

The letters spell out GILGAMESH, the name of the legendary king of Uruk
in ancient Sumer. The Epic of Gilgamesh is the name given to the whole text,
which is thought to be the oldest-surviving piece of notable literature.

- G – The immortal Utnapishtim tells the hero of how he gained his
  eternal life
- I – Five of the great gods had hatched a secret plan to bring about
  the destruction of humankind
- L – One of those gods, Ea, told Utnapishtim about the plan, which
  would take the form of a giant flood
- G – He told Utnapishtim to dismantle his house and build a boat
  in which he could escape the flood, along with several other living
  creatures
- A – The boat was to have very specific dimensions, and was made
  with wood, oil and bitumen
- M – Utnapishtim loaded the boat with his wife and relatives, food and
  provisions, and as many living animals as he could
- E – The gods then sent their secret storm, which raged for six days
  and six nights, destroying humanity and shattering the earth 'like a pot'
- S – After the storm, Utnapishtim sailed until he could find land, setting
  his livestock free and gaining the attention of the gods
- H – After some initial anger that a living being had survived the
  extinction event, the gods eventually bestowed immortality on
  Utnapishtim and his wife, who were transported to the mouth of
  the river Euphrates to live there for ever

9. Characterful Creation

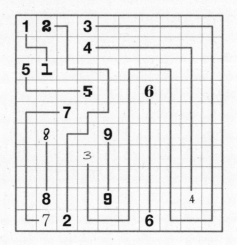

10. Cyrus's Cylinder

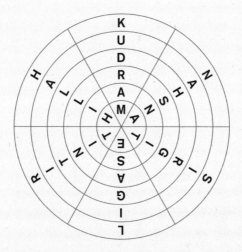

MARDUK – god loved by Cyrus, who helped him with his conquest

ANSHAN – ancient Persian city in which Cyrus was born and reigned over

TIGRIS – one of two ancient rivers of Mesopotamia, the other being Euphrates

ESAGIL – name of the Babylonian temple dedicated to the aforementioned god

TINTIR – traditional Sumerian name for Babylon

HILLAH – modern city in Iraq, on the site of ancient Babylon

11. Roman Occupations

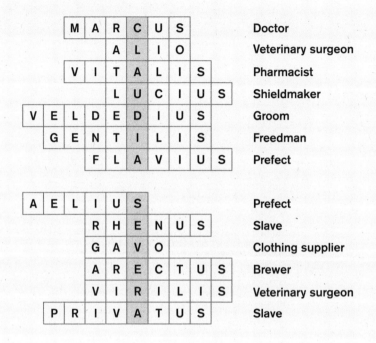

	M	A	R	C	U	S			Doctor
		A	L	I	O				Veterinary surgeon
	V	I	T	A	L	I	S		Pharmacist
		L	U	C	I	U	S		Shieldmaker
V	E	L	D	E	D	I	U	S	Groom
	G	E	N	T	I	L	I	S	Freedman
		F	L	A	V	I	U	S	Prefect

A	E	L	I	U	S			Prefect
	R	H	E	N	U	S		Slave
	G	A	V	O				Clothing supplier
	A	R	E	C	T	U	S	Brewer
	V	I	R	I	L	I	S	Veterinary surgeon
P	R	I	V	A	T	U	S	Slave

The name of the writer is Claudia Severa, who was wife of the Prefect Aelius Brocchus. Her personal note can be seen in the bottom-right of the image on the left-hand puzzle page.

12. Etruscan Enigma

The grid reads 'ETRUSCAN INSCRIPTIONS WERE OFTEN IN BOUSTROPHEDON STYLE' – and is itself written in boustrophedon style. 'Boustrophedon' is from the Greek meaning 'as an ox turns in ploughing' – that is, traversing from left to right across a field and then back again. So boustrophedon text reads first from left to right, and then from right to left again with mirrored lettering, then reverts to left to right, and so on. The message can therefore be interpreted like this:

E	T	R	U				
N	A	C	S	S	C	A	N
:	I	N	S				
P	I	R	C	C	R	I	P
T	I	O	N				
E	W	:	S	S	:	W	E
R	E	:	O				
N	E	T	F	F	T	E	N
:	I	N	:				
S	U	O	B	B	O	U	S
T	R	O	P				
O	D	E	H	H	E	D	O
N	:	S	T				
:	E	L	Y	Y	L	E	:

13. The Rosetta Stone

- Section 1 has been shifted forward four places, and therefore reads HIEROGLYPHIC SCRIPT USED BY PRIESTS.
- Section 2 has been shifted forward two places, and reads DEMOTIC SCRIPT FOR EVERYDAY WRITINGS
- Section 3 has been shifted forward seven places, and reads ALPHABETIC GREEK FOR ADMINISTRATION

14. The Crossword Block

	1	2	3	4
1→	A	M	O	N
2→	M	A	D	I
3→	O	D	I	N
4→	N	I	N	E

	1	2	3	4	5
1→	E	G	Y	P	T
2→	G	E	E	S	E
3→	Y	E	M	E	N
4→	P	S	E	U	D
5→	T	E	N	D	S

15. A List of Kings

The name which does not fit is HATSHEPSUT. Although a pharaoh of the prestigious 18th dynasty, Hatshepsut was a female pharaoh – and therefore apparently not considered a valid ruler by the pharaohs who succeeded her.

16. Ancient Problems

1.

| 10 | × 15 | +178 | − 12 | ÷100 | 3.16 |

2.

| 12 | × 5 | × 5 | + 10 | × 5 | 1550 |

3.

| 14 | × 4 | − 6 | × 2 | − 16 | 84 |

4.

| 16 | x 5 | ÷ 8 | × 5 | + 2 | 52 |

17. Ancient Games

IV	V	III	VI	II	I
II	VI	I	III	IV	V
III	II	V	I	VI	IV
I	IV	VI	V	III	II
V	III	IV	II	I	VI
VI	I	II	IV	V	III

18. Picture This

1.   May + A = Maya
2.   Pi + ram + ID = Pyramid
3.   M + 'A's = Maize
4.   Ewe + cat + AN = Yucatan

6 Treasures

1. The Palmerston Cups

- HE HAS NOT DESERVED SWEET UNLESS HE HAS TASTED BITTER
- SACRED TO THE DEPARTED
- THINK ON YOUR FRIENDS & DEATH AS THE CHIEF
- LET US DRINK TO THE DEAD

2. The Lycurgus Cup

- **GOLD** SOLD SOLE SALE **SAGE**
- **NAVY** NAVE PAVE PANE PINE **PINK**
- **BUFF** RUFF RIFF RIFE LIFE **LIME**
- **CYAN** CLAN CLAM SLAM SLUM **PLUM**

3. Medal Collection

Using the numbers on the puzzle pages, the coins should be placed in the following chronological order:

8 (V) – 2 (O) – 6 (T) – 7 (E) – 13 (S) – 11 (F) – 4 (O) – 12 (R) – 10 (W) – 3 (O) – 9 (M) – 5 (E) – 1 (N)

The message revealed is therefore VOTES FOR WOMEN, which was illegally overstamped on to several coins during the suffragette movement at the turn of the 20th century, including this example:

4. The Hoxne Hoard

The approximate translation of the message is therefore USE THIS HAPPILY, LADY JULIANA.

5. The Thetford Hoard 1

- 1× GEM – 1× BOX
- 3× BEAD – 22× RING
- 4× BRACELET – 5× NECKLACE
- 4× PENDANT – 1× AMULET
- 3× STRAINER – 33× SPOON

6. The Thetford Hoard 2

The word which uses all the letters is AMETHYST – the ring's central stone.

Other words to find include: ahem, ash, ashy, ate, aye, ayes, east, easy, eat, eats, eta, ham, hams, has, haste, hasty, hat, hate, hates, hats, hay, hays, heat, heats, mash, mast, mat, mate, mates, matey, maths, mats, matte, mattes, may, meat, meats, meaty, mesa, same, sat, sate, say, sea, seam, seat, sham, shame, state, stay, steam, steamy, tam, tame, tames, tamest, tams, taste, tasty, tat, tea, team, teams, teas, teat, teats, that, theta, yam, yams, yea, yeas and yeast.

7. Ædwen's Brooch

The links can be solved as follows:

- ME, to form CHIME and MEDIAL
- MAY, to form DISMAY and MAYBE
- THE, to form SEETHE and THEREIN
- LORD, to form WARLORD and LORDSHIP
- OWN, to form TUMBLEDOWN and OWNSOME
- HER, to form RATHER and HERRING

The first line is therefore "Ædwen owns ME, MAY THE LORD OWN HER". The rest of the inscription goes on to read, "May the Lord curse him who takes me from her, unless she gives me of her own free will."

8. The Royal Gold Cup

AGNES – Medieval saint depicted in enamel

PEARL – Precious gemstone used for embellishment

TUDOR – Stylized rose type depicted on the stem

LATIN – Language of the inscription

SPAIN – Country where the cup spent 300 years

BASSE – '_____-taille', enamelling technique

9. The Hedwig Beakers

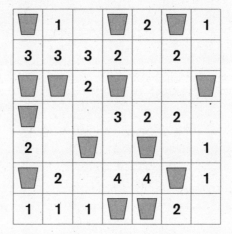

There are 14 beakers in the grid – which is therefore the number of known, complete Hedwig glasses.

10. The Jewels of Ur

The threaded beads are as follows:

Therefore the materials are AGATE, CARNELIAN, GOLD, LAPIS LAZULI and SILVER.

11. The Qianlong Bi

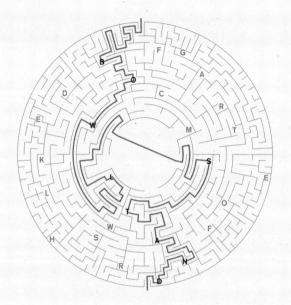

The letters spell BOWLSTAND – that is, 'bowl stand'. The first line of the inscription can be approximately translated as follows: 'It is said there were no bowls in antiquity / but if so then where did this stand come from?'.

12. The Mold Cape

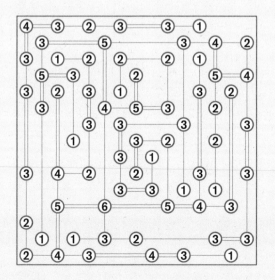

13. The Olduvai Stone Chopping Tool

- The stone used is BASALT, a volcanic rock
- The cutting edge was made with another, harder stone, used as a HAMMER
- This stone was uncovered in the country now known as TANZANIA
- A series of EARTHQUAKES has gradually exposed buried artefacts in the region
- It may have been used for obtaining BONE MARROW, an essential food source
- The tools were likely made by a HUMAN species similar to our own
- Tools of this kind are the earliest examples of TECHNOLOGY

Image Captions and Credits

The publisher would like to thank the copyright holders for granting permission to reproduce the images illustrated. Every attempt has been made to trace accurate ownership of copyrighted images in this book. Any errors or omissions will be corrected in subsequent editions provided notification is sent to the publisher.

Further information about the Museum and its collection can be found at britishmuseum. org. Descriptions and registration numbers of British Museum objects illustrated are included in the list below, arranged by page number. All are © 2023 The Trustees of the British Museum, courtesy the Department of Photography and Imaging, unless otherwise stated below.

Front and back cover (top to bottom): A circular game board of pale yellow limestone, Early Dynastic, Egypt, 1961,0408.1; Burnished black Bucchero pottery kantharos, 625–550 BCE, Italy, 1953,0426.1; Amulet in the form of a killer whale, bone, date unknown, Northwest Coast Peoples, North America, Am1976,03.21; Head of Hadrian, bronze, 117–138 CE, UK, 1848,1103.1; Comb in the form of a mermaid holding a skull, cow horn, 1980s, Mexico, Am1986,06.296; Red-figured stamnos (jar) with lid, depicting Herakles and the Lernian Hydra, pottery, c. 480–470 BCE, Greece, 1929,0513.1; *Rape of Europa* by Francesco Bartolozzi, print on paper, c. 1764–1802, UK, Ii,3.179. Donated by Thomas Thane; The Gayer-Anderson Cat, bronze, Late Period, Egypt, 1947,1011.1. Donated by Maj Robert Grenville Gayer-Anderson; Bowl decorated with two fish inside the bowl, 100 BCE–650 CE, Peru, Am1939,24.3; Kneeling figure of Horus of Pe, bronze, after 600 BCE, Egypt, 1880,0210.4; Standing cup, in the form of a unicorn, silver-gilt and chased, 1579–1898, Germany, WB.140. Bequeathed by Baron Ferdinand Anselm Rothschild; Pendant in the shape of a bird (probably an owl), jade, c. 3500 BCE, China, 1973,0726.116. Bequeathed by Brenda Zara Seligman; Turquoise mosaic of a double-headed serpent, 1400–1521, Mexico, Am1894,-.634. Christy Collection; Amulet-ring, silver, 17th century, place unknown, SLRings.83. Bequeathed by Sir Hans

Sloane; Nickel-bronze coin, 2000, Spain, 2005,1052.26. Donated by Anonymous; Finger ring, gold, c. 1370–1330 BCE, Egypt, 1839,0921.1095; Badge representing the legendary siren Melusine, metal, c. 16th–17th century, Europe, 1868,0120.8; Copper alloy coin, 221–210 BCE, Tunisia, 2013,4030.181. Donated by John Morcom; The Hunters' Palette, mudstone, Naqada III, Egypt, 1888,0512.65; Figure of Krishna playing the flute, stone, date unknown, India, As1977,04.31

6. Left to right: Amulet-ring, silver, 17th century, place unknown, SLRings. 83. Bequeathed by Sir Hans Sloane; Kneeling figure of Horus of Pe, bronze, after 600 BCE, Egypt, 1880,0210.4; The Hunters' Palette, mudstone, Naqada III, Egypt, 1888,0512.65; Finger ring, gold, c. 1370–1330 BCE, Egypt, 1839,0921.1095; Burnished black Bucchero pottery kantharos, 625–550 BCE, Italy, 1953,0426.1

7. Left to right: Figure of Krishna playing the flute, stone, date unknown, India, As1977,04.31; Turquoise mosaic of a double-headed serpent, 1400–1521, Mexico, Am1894,-.634. Christy Collection; *Rape of Europa* by Francesco Bartolozzi, print on paper, c. 1764–1802, UK, Ii,3.179. Donated by Thomas Thane; Amulet in the form of a killer whale, bone, date unknown, Northwest Coast Peoples, North America, Am1976,03.21; Bowl decorated with two fish inside the bowl, 100 BCE – 650 CE, Peru, Am1939,24.3; A circular game board of pale yellow limestone, Early Dynastic, Egypt, 1961,0408.1; Comb in the form of a mermaid holding a skull, cow horn, 1980s, Mexico, Am1986,06.296; The Gayer-Anderson Cat, bronze, Late Period, Egypt, 1947,1011.1. Donated by Maj Robert Grenville Gayer-Anderson

11. *The Progress of Civilisation*, original design by Sir Richard Westmacott for the group of sculptures in the pediment of the portico of the British Museum, brush drawing in brown wash, with pen and brown ink and watercolour, over black chalk, pre-1847, UK, 1887,0502.1

17. A. Changsha model of a bell, stoneware, 700–900 CE, China, PDF.327 | B. Postcard, c. 1900–1914, Algeria, EPH-ME.2200 | C. *A King's*

Ship Dressed with the Colours of different Nations, colour etching and aquatint with additional hand-colouring, 1794, UK, 1917,1208.4572. Donated by Nan Ino Cooper, Baroness Lucas of Crudwell, and Lady Dingwall, in memory of Auberon Thomas Herbert, 9th Baron Lucas of Crudwell and 5th Lord Dingwall | D. Cowrie moneta, with hole in back, collected in 1796, West Africa, SSB,155.4. Donated by Dorothea, Lady Banks | E. Model of a woman in the bath, terracotta, *c.* 450 BCE, Greece, 1864,1007.1935 | F. Unblown egg in two pieces, inscribed on the exterior in Arabic with black ink, Ottoman Dynasty, 1281–1924, Egypt, 1990,0127.377. Donated by Egypt Exploration Society

18.   Decorated stone sarcophagus and lid, carved in relief, early 4th century CE, UK, 1853,0620.1. Donated by Rev Thomas Hill and John Gay

19.   A. Pestle, stone, early 19th century, Caribbean, Am,+.4388. Donated by Sir Augustus Wollaston Franks | B. Part of a gold and silver clasp, 650–600 BCE, Italy, 1872,0604.1028 | C. Nickel-bronze coin, 2000, Spain, 2005,1052.26. Donated by Anonymous | D. A woman's apron (zastor), linen, 1900–1925, Croatia, Eu1997,04.6. Donated by Ken Ward | E. Chased gold brooch in the form of a camellia with the flowers of finely carved and tinted ivory, *c.* 1860, UK, 1978,1002.872. Donated by Anne Hull Grundy and Professor John Hull Grundy | F. Tassel, imitated in gold foil and flattened, 13th century BCE, Turkey, 1922,0511.376

24.   The Townley Discobolus, marble, 2nd century CE, Italy, 1805,0703.43

28.   Left: Military tombstone of Gaius Saufeius, limestone, 1st century CE, UK, 1873,0521.1 | Right: Military tombstone of Titus Valerius Pudens, limestone, 1st century CE, UK, 1853,1108.1. Donated by Arthur Trollope

32.   A. Set of mahjong tiles, bone, bamboo, pigment, 1800–1900, China, As1908,0416.1.b. Donated by Mrs M. Langenbach | B. The Lewis Chessmen, walrus ivory, *c.* 1150–1200, UK, 1831,1101.131 | C. Beadwork gaming board for pachisi, glass and cotton, *c.* 1850–1900,

India, As1959,12.1. Donated by Mrs M.C. Kenward | D. Black-figured amphora, pottery, *c.* 530 BCE, Greece, 1851,0806.15 | E. Ivory game-board/box for senet, *c.* 1400–1200 BCE, Egypt, 1965,0213.1 | F. Wari-board, carved of wood, early 20th century, Sierra Leone, Af1958,13.12. Donated by Mrs M. Addison | G. The Royal Game of Ur, wood and shell, 2600–2400 BCE, Iraq, 1928,1009.378 | H. A circular game board of pale yellow limestone, Early Dynastic, Egypt, 1961,0408.1 | I. Sugoroku of the Four Ranks board game, woodblock printed on paper, 18th century, Japan, 1896,0501,0.1742. Bequeathed by Lady Charlotte Schreiber

33.   The Lewis Chessmen, walrus ivory, *c.* 1150–1200, UK, 1831,1101.131

36.   Left: The Elgin Amphora, pottery, 760–750 BCE, Greece, 2004,0927.1. Purchased with contribution from Caryatid Fund, Art Fund (as NACF), British Museum Friends, Alexander Talbot Rice and Society of Dilettanti (Charitable Fund) | Right: Pitcher, pottery, 760–750 BCE, Greece, 1878,0812.8

38, 39.
      The Sophilos Dinos, pottery, 580–570 BCE, Greece, 1971,1101.1

40.   Clay tablet, 1750 BCE, Iraq, 1953,0411.71

42.   Brass hunting calendar, 1600–1620, Germany, WB.228. Bequeathed by Baron Ferdinand Anselm Rothschild

45.   From top: Miniature chocolate- or coffee-cup and saucer, lead-glazed earthenware, 1726–1775, UK, 1923,0122.33.CR. Bequeathed by Francis William Smith, donated through Art Fund (as NACF) | Yellow glaze parallel-sided stoneware teacup, 16th century, Japan, 1992,0525.31. Donated by Johannes Nikolaus Schmitt and Mareta Meade | Cup and saucer, enamelled porcelain, *c.* 1700, Japan, Franks.1099. Donated by Sir Augustus Wollaston Franks | Coffee cup, stonepaste ceramic, late 17th century, Iran, G.421. Bequeathed by Miss Edith Godman

47.   Head of Hadrian, bronze, 117–138 CE, UK, 1848,1103.1

48. Top left: Mould-pressed mosaic
glass dish, 225–200 BCE, Eastern
Mediterranean, 1871,0518.3.
Bequeathed by Felix Slade | Top right:
Hemispherical mould-pressed mosaic
glass bowl, 200–100 BCE, Eastern
Mediterranean, 1849,1121.1 | Centre
left: Hemispherical mould-pressed
mosaic glass bowl, 200–100 BCE,
Italy, 1873,0820.421 | Centre right:
Hemispherical mould-pressed mosaic
glass bowl, 200–100 BCE, Italy,
1847,1101.25. Donated by Campanari
| Bottom left: Hemispherical mould-
pressed millefiori glass bowl, 300–150
BCE, Italy, 1873,0820.419 | Bottom
right: Cast mosaic glass bowl, 200–50
BCE, Hellenistic, 1836,0224.488

50. Top: Navigation chart (rebbelib), made
of shells bound to palm-leaf sticks with
bast strings, date unknown, Marshall
Islands, Oc1944,02.931. Donated by
Irene Marguerite Beasley | Bottom left:
Navigation chart (rebbelib), made of
cane, fibre and shells, 19th century,
Marshall Islands, Oc1904,0621.34
| Bottom right: Navigation chart of
straight and curved slivers of light
wood tied in position, 19th–20th
century, Marshall Islands, Oc1941,01.4.
Donated by Irene Marguerite Beasley

52. Wool sock for the left foot of a child,
3rd–4th century, Egypt, 1914,1010.15.
Donated by Egypt Exploration Fund

53. Citole, wood and silver gilt, c. 1280–
1300, UK, 1963,1002.1. Purchased
with assistance from Art Fund and the
Pilgrim Trust

54. Cup, pottery, 1700–1600 BCE, Greece,
1950,1106.6. Donated by Miss E.I.
Salvage

57. A. Small ceramic bowl containing
several sun-dried fish and a strip
of textile, date unknown, Egypt,
1877,1112.48 | B. Offering-stand
holding cooked duck and loaves of
bread, wicker, 18th Dynasty, Egypt,
1837,0714.43 | C. Food product,
pastry, mid-8th century, China,
1928,1022.123 | D. Three-cornered
loaf of bread, New Kingdom, Egypt,
1904,1008.42. Donated by Egypt
Exploration Fund | E. Charred figs
and pieces of bread, survivals from
the eruption of Vesuvius over Pompeii,

79 CE, Italy, 1772,0311.92-93 | F. Food
product, pastry, c. 701–750 CE, China,
1928,1022.127

59. A. The Lion of Knidos, marble, 2nd
century BCE, Turkey, 1859,1226.24 |
B. Monumental scarab beetle, probably
representing Khepri, diorite, 4th century
BCE, probably from Heliopolis, Egypt,
.74 | C. Statue from the Mausoleum
of Halikarnassos, marble, c. 350 BCE,
Turkey, 1857,1220.238

61. A. Life-size figure of an Indian
terrapin, green nephrite, c. 1600, India,
1830,0612.1. Donated through James
Nairne, Esq. from Thomas Wilkinson
| B. Lion head finial, gypsum, 2500
BCE, Iraq, .91879 | C. Pendant in the
shape of a bird (probably an owl), jade,
c. 3500 BCE, China, 1973,0726.116.
Bequeathed by Brenda Zara Seligman
| D. Figure of a hippopotamus,
pottery, 1st or 2nd Dynasty, Egypt,
1903,1010.37. Donated by Egypt
Exploration Fund | E. Figure of a bird,
lapiz lazuli, date unknown, China,
1902,1220.155. Donated by British
Collection of Central Asian Antiquities
| F. Figure of a camel's head, plaster,
Abbasid dynasty, 749–1258, Iraq,
OA+.10978 | G. The Gayer-Anderson
Cat, bronze, Late Period, Egypt,
1947,1011.1. Donated by Maj Robert
Grenville Gayer-Anderson

63. Book of the Dead of Hunefer, frame
3, papyrus, 19th Dynasty, Egypt,
1852,0525.1.3

65. Top: Badge representing the legendary
siren Melusine, metal, c. 16th–17th
century, Europe, 1868,0120.8 | Centre:
Comb in the form of a mermaid holding
a skull, cow horn, 1980s, Mexico,
Am1986,06.296 | Bottom: Standing
cup, in the form of a unicorn, silver-gilt
and chased, 1579–1898, Germany,
WB.140. Bequeathed by Baron
Ferdinand Anselm Rothschild

67. A. Oak wreath with a bee and
two cicadas, gold, 350–300 BCE,
Turkey, 1908,0414.1 | B. Ceres by
Jacopo Caraglio, engraving on paper,
1526, Italy, 1866,0407.831 | C.
Figure of a lion, bronze, c. 510 BCE,
Greece, 1913,1113.6 | D. Black-
figured kantharos with donkey-head
attachment, pottery, 520–500 BCE,

Greece, 1876,0328.5 | E. *Rape of Europa* by Francesco Bartolozzi, print on paper, c. 1764–1802, UK, Ii,3.179. Donated by Thomas Thane | F. Body sherd of Chian Mature Animal Style pottery chalice, pottery, c. 610–580 BCE, Greece, 1886,0401.1075. Donated by Egypt Exploration Fund

68. The Hunters' Palette, mudstone, Naqada III, Egypt, 1888,0512.65

71. A. Figure of Anubis as a standing jackal-headed figure wearing armlets, bracelets and anklets, bronze, Late Period, Egypt, .61010 | B. Seated statue of Sekhmet, granodiorite, 18th Dynasty (statue), 20th Dynasty (inscription), Egypt, .63 | C. Figure of Sobek, bronze, Ptolemaic or Late Period, Egypt, 1891,0511.20 | D. Kneeling figure of Horus of Pe, bronze, after 600 BCE, Egypt, 1880,0210.4

73. A. Amulet in form of turtle, stone, Mesopotamian, Iraq, 1929,1017.429 | B. Animal, probably a dog of which the head, neck and forepaws are preserved, fired clay, 700–500 BCE, Iraq, 1854,0401.32 | C. Tiger, marble, c. 1200–1050 BCE, China, 1949,0712.1. Donated by Miss M. Hambleton | D. Brooch in the form of a butterfly, tortoiseshell, c. 1840–1870, Sri Lanka, 1978,1002.203. Donated by Anne Hull Grundy and Professor John Hull Grundy | E. Articulated figure (jizai okimono) of a catfish, iron, 1701–1850, Japan, 1948,0414.1. Donated by C.G. Davies | F. Hollow-cast figure of the Apis Bull wearing the sun-disc and uraeus, copper alloy, Late Period, Egypt, OC.557 | G. Head of a figure of a cow, calcite, c. 1450 BCE, Egypt, 1905,1014.7. Donated by Egypt Exploration Fund

74. A. Toy, in the shape of a dachshund, carved walnut, 1934, Denmark, 2014,8024.253 | B. Painted rooster figure, pottery, date unknown, Sri Lanka, As1984,22.133 | C. Vessel in the shape of a camelid (possibly llama or alpaca), pottery, 200–600 CE, Peru, Am1933,0713.58. Donated by Dame Clarissa Reid | D. Groundhog, illustration to an unidentified Latin edition of Sebastian Münster, *Cosmographia*, paper, 1544–1552,

Switzerland, 1982, U.2547 | E. Eagle figure made of andesite, c. 1300–1521, Mexico, Am.8624 | F. The Swimming Reindeer, mammoth ivory, 11,000 BCE, France, Palart.550. Funded by Christy Fund

75. Top: Turquoise mosaic of a double-headed serpent, 1400–1521, Mexico, Am1894,-.634. Christy Collection | Bottom: Kozo, double-headed dog, wood, c. 1900 CE century, Kongo, Democratic Republic of Congo, Af1905,0525.6

77. Amulets of the Sons of Horus, glazed composition, c. 1069–747 BCE, Egypt, 1895,0511.11-14

79. A. *Des Chats. Dessins sans paroles par Steinlen* by Theophile Alexandre Steinlen, lithograph on paper, 1898, France, 1949,0411.4999.1-26. Bequeathed by Campbell Dodgson | B. Cat looking through lattice window at rice fields near Asakusa by Utagawa Hiroshige, colour woodblock print on paper, 1857, Japan, 1906,1220,0.664 | C. Sheet of four proof images illustrating Lewis Carroll's *Alice's Adventures in Wonderland*, Daziel Brothers after Sir John Tenniel, wood-engraving on paper, 1865–1957, UK, 1957,0308.5 | D. *The Large Cat* by Cornelis Visscher, engraving on paper, c. 1657, The Netherlands, 1953,0411.89. Bequeathed by Edward Howard William Meyerstein

80–81.
The Big Fish Eat the Little Fish by Pieter van der Heyden after Pieter Bruegel the Elder, engraving on paper, 1557, The Netherlands, 1875,0710.2651

83. Dog figurines, fired clay, c. 645 BCE, Iraq, 1856,0903.1507

85. Panel from a mosaic floor, stone, c. 100 CE, Italy, 1989,0322.1

86. A. Amulet, gold, 1st century BCE, Libya, 1859,1222.2 | B. Amulet in the form of the frog-goddess Heket, diorite-gneiss, New Kingdom or Third Intermediate Period, Egypt, 1881,0614.137 | C. Amulet in the form of a fish, coral, 17th–18th century, production place unknown, 2003,0331.20

87. A. Amulet in the form of a recumbent bull wearing horned head-dress,

lapis lazuli, date unknown, Asia, 1909,0510.10 | B. Amulet of a couchant bull, shell, 2600–2400 BCE, Iraq, 1928,1009.396 | C. Stamp-seal, amulet or model in form of a couchant animal, black hematite, 3000–2900 BCE, Iraq, 1924,0920.51 | D. Amulet in the form of two antelopes, gold, 2600 BCE, Iraq, 1928,1010.86 | E. Amuletic figure of a dog-faced baboon, glazed composition, c. 600 BCE, Egypt, 1946,1204.123. Donated by Mrs Marion Whiteford Acworth JP

89. A. Figure of a dog in harness, green glazed earthenware, c. 1st–2nd century CE, China, 1928,0118.1. Donated by Henry J. Oppenheim | B. Figure of dog with bronze fish in mouth, ivory, c. 1350–1300 BCE, Egypt, 1883,1018.99 | C. Figure of a dog with a hare in its mouth, terracotta, c. 600–580 BCE, Greece, 1909,0616.2 | D. The Townley Greyhounds, marble, 1st–2nd century CE, Italy, 1805,0703.8 | E. Dog votive figure, terracotta, 2000–1700 BCE, Greece, 1907,0119.57. Donated by British School at Athens | F. Jackal or dog on a plinth, limestone, 1st century BCE–2nd century CE, Egypt, 1924,0510.5 | G. Figure representing a dog, pottery, 300 BCE–300 CE, Mexico, Am1921,0613.1. Donated by Vice-Adm E Rooke | H. Animal figurine, copper alloy, c. 150–50 BCE, UK, 1864,0501.10

91. Top and Centre: Wall panel relief depicting lion hunt, gypsum, 645–635 BCE, North Palace, Nineveh, Iraq, 1856,0909.16 | Bottom: Wall panel relief showing Ashurnasirpal II hunting lions, gypsum, 865–860 BCE, North West Palace, Nimrud, Iraq, 1847,0623.11

93. A. Standing cup, nautilus shell mounted in silver, gilt and chased, c. 1550, Germany, WB.114. Bequeathed by Baron Ferdinand Anselm Rothschild | B. Standing cup, silver-gilt and chased, in the form of a rampant boar, c. 1620, Germany, WB.135. Bequeathed by Baron Ferdinand Anselm Rothschild | C. Standing cup, silver-gilt and chased, in the form of a bear seated on hind quarters and grasping a staff with its right paw, 1800–1898,

Germany, WB.139. Bequeathed by Baron Ferdinand Anselm Rothschild | D. Standing cup, silver-gilt and chased, in the form of a cock standing on one leg, 1825–1898, Germany, WB.141. Bequeathed by Baron Ferdinand Anselm Rothschild | E. Standing cup, silver-gilt and chased, in the form of a running stag resting its forefeet on a shield with a coat of arms, 1550–1600, Austria, WB.138. Bequeathed by Baron Ferdinand Anselm Rothschild | F. Standing cup, silver-gilt and chased, in the form of a unicorn, 1579–1898, Germany, WB.140. Bequeathed by Baron Ferdinand Anselm Rothschild

95. Necklace made of river dolphin teeth and plant fibres, pre-1925, Colombia, Am1925,0704.9. Donated by E. Seymour Bell

97. A. Amulet in the form of a killer whale, bone, date unknown, Northwest Coast Peoples, North America, Am1976,03.21 | B. Engraved pendant decorated on one side with a drawing of a wolverine, bone, late Magdalenian period, c. 14,000 to 10,000 years ago, France, Palart.102. Funded by Christy Fund | C. Armadillo-shaped vessel, pottery with beige, white and red polychrome, date unknown, Mexico, Am1936,1124.1. Donated by Mrs F.M. Horner | D. Coiled rattlesnake figure, granite, c. 1325–1521, Mexico, Am1849,0629.1 | E. Walrus figure, walrus ivory, date unknown, Aleutian Islands, Am1981,12.52. Donated by Wellcome Institute for the History of Medicine | F. Bead in form of a cuttlefish, steatite or picrolite, 3000 BCE–500 CE, Cyprus, 1966,1101.1

99. Mosaic mask of Tezcatlipoca, human skull covered with turquoise and lignite mosaic held in place with pine resin adhesive, 1400–1521, Mexico, Am,St.401. Donated by Henry Christy

100. Left: Fragment of the sarcophagus of Ramses VI, conglomerate, c. 1150 BCE, Egypt, .140 | Right: Sarcophagus of Pakap, basalt, 589–570 BCE or later, Egypt, 1907,1014.2

101. Coffin of Horaawesheb, painted wood, linen and human tissue, 22nd Dynasty, Egypt, .6666

102. Brooch engraved and carved with design in Northwest Coast style of

Thunderbird catching a whale, silver,
1953–1965, Canada, Am2000,02.1.
Donated by Mrs June Bedford in honour
of Jonathan C.H. King

103. Totem pole, cedar wood, c. 1850,
Haida, Northwest Coast Peoples,
Canada, Am1903,0314.1

105. Left: Model totem pole, argillite and
wood, pre-1897, Haida, Northwest
Coast Peoples, Canada, Am1897,-.8.
Donated by Sir Augustus Wollaston
Franks | Right: Totemic doorway
representing an eagle (or Thunderbird)
and the Raven, carved of wood, pre-
1897, Haida, Northwest Coast Peoples,
Canada, Am1958,02.1. Donated by
Royal Botanic Gardens, Kew

107. Top: Five beads in the form of eyes,
blue, yellow and white glass, date
unknown, Hebron, West Bank,
As1966,01.833. a-e | Bottom left:
Hand-shaped pendant, gilded copper
wire with a turquoise bead, 1900–
1930, Gaza, As1966,01.440 | Bottom
right: Necklace, blue, yellow and
white glass beads in the form of eyes,
date unknown, Hebron, West Bank,
As1966,01.832

108. Figure known as A'a, sandalwood, pre-
1821, Rurutu, Polynesia, Oc,LMS.19

111. Aramaic incantation bowl, pottery,
6th–8th century, Iraq, 1911,0408.49

113. A. Bronze figure of Athena, date
and production place unknown,
1873,0820.66 | B. Copper alloy coin,
221–210 BCE, Tunisia, 2013,4030.181.
Donated by John Morcom | C.
The Floating Bridge of Heaven by
Utagawa Hiroshige, colour woodblock
print on paper, 1847–1851, Japan,
1921,1115,0.2 | D. Figure of Satis or
Nekhbet, blue glazed composition,
Third Intermediate Period, Egypt,
1895,0511.21 | E. Left: Figure of
Taweret, blue glazed composition,
26th Dynasty, Egypt, 1946,1204.116;
Centre: Figure of Taweret, green glazed
composition (now white), 26th Dynasty,
Egypt, 1927,0514.24; Right: Figure
of Taweret, blue glazed steatite, Late
Period, Egypt, 1847,0807.2 | F. Dryad
by Cornelis Cort after Frans Floris,
engraving on paper, 1564,
The Netherlands, F,1.298 | G. Coin,
silver, c. 710 720, Afghanistan,

IOC.2361 | H. Cylinder seal, pink
calcite, 3000 BCE, Iraq, 1879,0115.1
| I. Left: Hope by Jacob Matham
after Hendrik Goltzius, engraving on
paper, c. 1593, The Netherlands,
1959,1201.12. Donated by Constance
Richardson; Centre: Hope by Jacob
Matham after Hendrik Goltzius,
engraving on paper, 1593, The
Netherlands, 1857,0613.504; Right:
Hope by Anonymous, engraving on
paper, 1520–1550, Italy, 1993,U.10.
Bequeathed by Clayton Mordaunt
Cracherode

114. Magical mirror, wax discs, gold disc
and rock crystal ball associated with
Dr Dee, late 16th century, Mexico and
unknown, wax discs 1838,1232.90.
a–c. Donated by Sir John Cotton,
3rd Baronet; gold disc 1942,0506.1.
Donated by Art Fund; magical mirror
1966,1001.1; rock crystal ball
SLCups.232. Bequeathed by Sir
Hans Sloane

115. Rock crystal ball associated with
Dr Dee, 17th century, place unknown,
SLCups.232. Bequeathed by Sir
Hans Sloane

116. Left: Miniature altar, wood with
pottery offerings, 1970s, Mexico,
Am1978,15.630 | Right: Figurine of
La Catrina, pottery, 1980s, Mexico,
Am1990,08.157

117. Top: Comb, carved from cow horn,
1980s, Mexico, Am1986,06.299
| Bottom left: Figurine, sugar in
the form of skull, 1980s, Mexico,
Am1989,12.449 | Bottom right:
Miniature candelabrum in the form
of a tree of life, varnished pottery,
1980s, Mexico, Am1989,12.193.a

119. Top left: Papercut, gold foil paper,
1980s, Mexico, Am1990,08.536 | Top
right: Papercut, gold foil paper, 1980s,
Mexico, Am1990,08.534 | Bottom
left: Papercut, gold foil paper, 1980s,
Mexico, Am1990,08.538 | Bottom right:
Banner, tissue paper, 1980s, Mexico,
Am1986,06.497

121. Top: Figure of Krishna playing the
flute, stone, date unknown, India,
As1977,04.31 | Centre: Amulet
depicting elephant-headed Hindu
god Ganesha, silver, pre-1865, India,
1865,0803.01 | Bottom: Calling card

case decorated with a seated figure of Ganesha in high repoussé, surrounded by a floral Kutch scroll, silver, c. 1880, India, 2011,3014.9. Bequeathed by Oppi Untracht

123. A. Bird mask, wood, pre-1939, Canada, Am1976,03.7. Donated by Dr Robert Bruce Inverarity | B. Painted mask (tapuanu), breadfruit wood, coconut fibre cord and natural pigments, 19th century, Micronesia, Oc1944,02.943. Donated by Irene Marguerite Beasley | C. Mask for bugaku performance, lacquered and gilt wood, 17th century, Japan, 1978,0421.2.a | D. Mask with rings and appendages, wood, dog teeth, sinew, root and feather, 1940s, Yupiit, Nunivak Island, Alaska, USA, Am1976,03.79.b-m | E. Mourning mask, carved in wood and adorned with human hair, pre-1853, Kanak, Melanesia, Oc1954,06.260. Donated by Wellcome Institute for the History of Medicine

125. Amulet with Hebrew text, silver, 18th century, Middle East, 1867,0709.5. Donated by Rev Greville John Chester

128–129.
A. Illustrations from Lucian's True History translated by Frances Hickes top: by William Strang, bottom: by J.B. Clark, photorelief on paper, 1894, UK, 1960,0430.5 | B. Painting of the snake-goddess Manasā in the Madhubani Style, unknown artist, paint on paper, 1965–1972, India, 2000,1012,0.16. Donated by Dr Achinto Sen-Gupta | C. Saito Oniwaka-maru, the young Benkei, fighting the carp in the water by Utagawa Kuniyoshi, woodblock print on paper, mid-19th century, Japan, 2008,3037.21217. Donated by American Friends of the British Museum | D. Tametomo and his son rescued by tengu by Utagawa Kuniyoshi after Katsushika Hokusai, colour woodblock-printed triptych on paper, 1848–1852, Japan, 1906,1220,0.1339

131. Top: Black-figured kyathos, pottery, c. 500 BCE, Greece, 1847,0806.45 | Centre: Cylinder seal, serpentinite, 900–750 BCE, Asia, 1896,0619.1 | Bottom: Proof illustration to Pope's The Iliad of Homer, James Heath after

Henry Howard, etching and engraving on paper, 1805, UK, 1875,0710.3417

133. Left: Rubbing of a Han dynasty stone relief decorated with the mythical deity Fuxi, paper, 1980–2010, China, 2013,3011.59. Donated by Dame Jessica Rawson | Right: Stone plaque with the figure of a five-headed cobra (nagakal), 17th century, India, 1900,1011.1

136. A. Amulet-ring, gold, 13th century, place unknown, AF.1020. Bequeathed by Sir Augustus Wollaston Franks | B. Amulet-ring, silver, 17th century, place unknown, SLRings.83. Bequeathed by Sir Hans Sloane | C. Finger ring, gold, 8th–10th century, UK, OA.10262. Donated by George Hamilton Gordon, 4th Earl of Aberdeen | D. Amulet-ring, gold, 14th century, place unknown, AF.1000. Bequeathed by Sir Augustus Wollaston Franks | E. Finger ring, gold, c. 1370–1330 BCE, Egypt, 1839,0921.1095 | F. Warrior's ring, brass, 1850–1930, Indonesia, As1933,0307.8 | G. Amulet-ring, gold, 14th century, Italy, AF.1023. Bequeathed by Sir Augustus Wollaston Franks | H. Amulet-ring, bronze, 17th century, place unknown, OA.7467

137. Amulet, pendant, brass, 16th–18th century, Europe, OA.1373 (see also p. 230)

139. Top: ArtMarie/istockphoto.com | Centre left: Bowl with polychrome painting of demon on both sides, pottery, 100 BCE–600 CE, Peru, Am1941,04.48. Donated by Lady Dow Steel-Maitland | Centre right: Beaker, pottery, 100 BCE–600 CE, Peru, Am1930,0712.3 | Bottom: Textile, wool, 200 BCE–600 CE, Peru, Am1954,05.616. Donated by Wellcome Institute for the History of Medicine

141. Gypsum tablet showing archaic numerals, 3300–3100 BCE, Iraq, 1851,0101.217

142. Marble votive inscription dedicated by Antonius, a libertus or freed slave, 193–211 CE, Italy, 1805,0703.210

144–145.
The Admonitions Scroll, silk and paper, 5th–7th century, China, 1903,0408,0.1

147. A. Perfume-bottle modelled as a lion, terracotta, 625–575 BCE, Italy,

1852,0112.8 | B. Agate finger ring, 8th–10th century, Anglo-Saxon, c. 400–1000 CE, 1873,0210.3. Donated by Sir Augustus Wollaston Franks | C. Etruscan helmet of the Negau type, bronze, c. 474 BCE, Italy, 1823,0610.1. Donated by George IV, King of the United Kingdom | D. Stele with inscription dedicating stele and oil lamp to the rustic god Silvanus, marble, 1st century, Italy, 1986,0405.1 | E. Box-shaped metal pendant, amulet, 16th–18th century, Europe, OA.1365

149, 150.
The Franks Casket, whalebone, early 8th century, France, 1867,0120.1. Donated by Sir Augustus Wollaston Franks

153. Upper part of a clay tablet, 7th century BCE, Iraq, K.43

155. The Flood Tablet, clay, 7th century BCE, Iraq, K.3375

156. Jade book, 1748, China, As.3573. Donated by Henry Christy

159. The Cyrus Cylinder, clay, after 539 BCE, Iraq, 1880,0617.1941

160. Writing tablet, party invitation written in ink, wood, 97–103 CE, UK, 1986,1001.64

161. Left: Writing tablet, five lines of a letter written in ink, wood, Roman Britain, 43–410 CE, UK, 1986,1001.105 | Right: Writing tablet, five fragments of official document, written in ink on both sides, wood, Roman Britain, 43–410 CE, UK, 1980,0303.3

162. Top: Burnished black Bucchero pottery kantharos, 625–550 BCE, Italy, 1953,0426.1 | Bottom: Part of a copper alloy plaque with Etruscan inscription, 3rd–2nd century BCE, Italy 2007,8045.225

165. The Rosetta Stone, granodiorite, 196 BCE, Egypt, .24. Donated by George III, King of the United Kingdom

166, 167.
The 'Crossword' Stela of Peser, limestone, 20th Dynasty, Egypt, .194

169. Part of a limestone king-list comprising 34 names, c. 1250 BCE, Egypt, .117

171. The Rhind Mathematical Papyrus, c. 1550 BCE, Egypt, 1865,0218.3

173. Top: Flat circular rock crystal game-counter, inscribed with the number fifteen in Greek and Roman numerals,

1st–2nd century, place unknown, 1923,0401.47 | Middle: Flat circular rock crystal game-counter, inscribed with the number four in Greek and Roman numerals, 1st–2nd century, place unknown, 1923,0401.22 | Bottom: Flat circular rock crystal game-counter, inscribed XIIII, 1st–2nd century, Italy, 1890,0921.16

175. The Yaxchilan Lintels, carved limestone lintel, showing Lady K'ab'al Xook on the bottom right of the panel, c. 725 CE, Mexico, Am1923,Maud.5

177. The Palmerston Gold Chocolate Cups, c. 1700, UK, 2005,0604.2

179. The Lycurgus Cup, glass, 4th century, probably made in Rome, 1958,1202.1. Purchased with contribution from Art Fund (as NACF)

180. 1. Bronze medal, 1760, Switzerland, 1947,0607.145. Donated by Doctor Sidney Fairbairn | 2. Bronze medal, c. 1731, UK, G3,EMDass.2. Donated by George IV, King of the United Kingdom | 3. Silver medal, c. 1731, Switzerland, G3,EM.204. Donated by George IV, King of the United Kingdom | 4. Silver medal, c. 1731, Switzerland, M.6765 | 5. Bronze medal, c. 1731, UK, 1947,0607.148. Donated by Doctor Sidney Fairbairn | 6. Copper medal, c. 1731, UK, M.6762

181. 7. Copper medal, c. 1731, UK, M.6763 | 8. Bronze medal, c. 1731, UK, G3,EMDass.1. Donated by George IV, King of the United Kingdom | 9. Bronze medal, c. 1731, UK, 1865,0324.1609. Donated by Bank of England | 10. Bronze medal, c. 1731, Switzerland, BNK,EngM.650. Donated by Bank of England | 11. Silver medal, c. 1731, UK, M.6764. Bequeathed by Clayton Mordaunt Cracherode | 12. Bronze medal, c. 1731, UK, BNK,EngM.649. Donated by Bank of England | 13. Bronze medal, c. 1731, UK, G3,EMDass.18. Donated by George IV, King of the United Kingdom | Bottom right: Suffragette defaced penny, 1903, UK, 1991,0733.1. Donated by R. Johnson (see also p. 241)

183. Gold pierced bracelet with inscription to Juliane, Roman Britain, 43–410 CE, UK, 1994,0408.29. Purchased with contribution from Art Fund (as NACF),

National Heritage Memorial Fund and
British Museum Friends (as British
Museum Society)

185. Buckle, gold, Roman Britain, 4th
century CE, UK, 1981,0201.1

186. Gold ring with shoulders in the form
of dolphins and a large flat bezel with
settings for nine stones, Roman Britain,
43–410 CE, UK, 1981,0201.5

187. The Aedwen Brooch, silver, early 11th
century, UK, 1951,1011.1

189. The Royal Gold Cup, made of gold
and enamel, c. 1370–1380, France,
1892,0501.1. Purchased with
contribution from the Worshipful
Company of Goldsmiths, HM Treasury
and private donations

190. Hedwig beaker, glass, 12th century,
East Mediterranean or Sicily,
1959,0414.1. Funded by P.T. Brooke
Sewell, Esq.

192. Cylindrical beads and leaf pendants,
gold, cornelian and lapis lazuli,
2600–2500 BCE, Iraq, 1928,1010.107

193. Top left: Necklace of 64 beads
and pendants, lapis lazuli, gold and
cornelian, 2600–2500 BCE, Iraq,
1928,1009.67 | Top right: Group of
3 lapis lazuli and 1 banded agate
beads, ending in a pendant in the form
of a recumbent bull, 2600 BCE, Iraq,
1928,1010.103 | Centre: Necklace
of 80 beads, cornelian and lapis
lazuli, 2600 BCE, Iraq, 1929,1017.260
| Bottom left: Lapis lazuli beads,
biconical, carved, perforated,
and polished, 2600 BCE, Iraq,
1928,1010.192 | Bottom right: String of
beads, gold, lapiz lazuli and cornelian,
2600 BCE, Iraq, 1929,1017.122

194. Jade collared ring (bi), 1200–1050 BCE,
China, 1937,0416.140

196. The Mold Gold Cape, c. 1900–1600
BCE, UK, 1836,0902.1. Donated by Rev
George Rushleigh

198. Chopping tool made of basalt,
1.2 million years old, Tanzania,
1934,1214.2. Purchased with
contribution from The British Museum,
Royal Geographical Society, Royal
Society and University of Cambridge

Acknowledgments

Writing a book that aims to include a representative sample of the many wonders on display at the British Museum is a complex task, so huge thanks are owed to Ben Hayes, Mark Ralph and the team at Thames & Hudson for their fantastic help throughout the editorial process and for ensuring the book looks incredible throughout. Thanks are also due, of course, to Claudia Bloch, Barrie Cook, Laura Meachem and everyone at the British Museum for their assistance. I am also heavily indebted to my colleague Laura Jayne Ayres, who has been instrumental in the writing of this book and without whose help it would have been a considerably more daunting project. And last, but absolutely not least, thank you so much to my wife, Sara, and my son, Theo, for your love and for all the times I've been too busy working to do anything else. I couldn't do it without you!

—Dr Gareth Moore

Dr Gareth Moore is the internationally bestselling author of a wide range of brain-training and puzzle books for both children and adults, including *The Mindfulness Puzzle Book*, *The Great British Puzzle Book*, *Stay Sharp!* and *The Ordnance Survey Puzzle Book*. His books have sold millions of copies in the UK alone, and have been published in more than thirty different languages. He is also the creator of online brain-training site BrainedUp.com, and runs the daily puzzle site PuzzleMix.com. Find him online at DrGarethMoore.com, on Twitter as @DrGarethMoore, and at YouTube.com/@DrGareth.